MAUS

Art Spiegelman

AUTHORED by Jack Murphy
UPDATED AND REVISED by Jordan Berkow

COVER DESIGN by Table XI Partners LLC
COVER PHOTO by Olivia Verma and © 2005 GradeSaver, LLC

BOOK DESIGN by Table XI Partners LLC

Published by GradeSaver LLC, www.gradesaver.com

First published in the United States of America by GradeSaver LLC. 2007

GRADESAVER, the GradeSaver logo and the phrase "Getting you the grade since 1999" are registered trademarks of GradeSaver, LLC

ISBN 978-1-60259-086-1

Printed in the United States of America

For other products and additional information please visit
http://www.gradesaver.com

Table of Contents

Biography of Art Spiegelman (1948–)..1

About MAUS...3

Character List...5

Major Themes...13

Glossary of Terms..19

Short Summary..23
    Book I: My Father Bleeds History..23
    Book II: And Here My Troubles Began...25

Summary and Analysis of Book I, Chapter 1...29
    The Sheik..29
    Analysis...30

Summary and Analysis of Book I, Chapter 2...33
    The Honeymoon...33
    Analysis...34

Summary and Analysis of Book I, Chapter 3...37
    Prisoner of War...37
    Analysis...38

Summary and Analysis of Book I, Chapter 4...41
    The Noose Tightens..41
    Analysis...43

Summary and Analysis of Book I, Chapter 5...45
    Mouse Holes...45
    Analysis...47

Summary and Analysis of Book I, Chapter 6...49
    Mouse Trap...49
    Analysis...51

Summary and Analysis of Book II, Chapter 1..53
    Mauschwitz...53
    Analysis...54

Table of Contents

Summary and Analysis of Book II, Chapter 2..57

    Auschwitz: Time Flies...57

    Analysis...59

Summary and Analysis of Book II, Chapter 3..63

    And Here My Troubles Began...63

    Analysis...65

Summary and Analysis of Book II, Chapter 4..67

    Saved..67

    Analysis...68

Summary and Analysis of Book II, Chapter 5..71

    The Second Honeymoon..71

    Analysis...72

Suggested Essay Questions...75

Questions of Genre in Maus..77

Author of ClassicNote and Sources..79

Essay: Stylistic Detail of MAUS and Its Effect on Reader Attachment............81

Essay: Using Animals to Divide: Illustrated Allegory in Maus and Terrible Things..85

Quiz 1..89

Quiz 1 Answer Key..95

Quiz 2..97

Quiz 2 Answer Key..103

Quiz 3..105

Quiz 3 Answer Key..111

Quiz 4..113

Quiz 4 Answer Key..119

Biography of Art Spiegelman (1948–)

Art Spiegelman is a critically acclaimed and highly influential artist and graphic novelist. He was born in Stockholm, Sweden, in 1948, and soon after immigrated with his parents to Rego Park, a neighborhood of Queens, NY. Though his parents wished for him to become a dentist, Spiegelman enrolled in Harpur College in upstate New York (now Binghamton University, part of the State University of New York) and began studying art and philosophy. He left college two years later in 1968 without a degree, following a nervous breakdown.

His early career as an artist began in 1966 at Topps Gum Company, where he drew "Bazooka Joe" comics and helped to create the cult classic "Garbage Pail Kids," which were drawn in a similar style to the popular "Cabbage Patch Kids" dolls but with gross – often vulgar – details. He worked at Topps for twenty years, until a dispute over the ownership of his original artworks caused him to leave.

During his time at Topps, he also began publishing his own artwork in underground magazines such as *Real Pulp* and *Bizarre Sex*. In 1980, Spiegelman founded *RAW* (*Real Art Works*), a magazine of unconventional comics, with his wife, the artist Francoise Mouly. The first volume of *Maus* was first published in serial form within the pages of *RAW* between 1980 and 1985, and was released as a book the following year, to enormous critical and popular success. After the second volume of *Maus* was published in 1992, Spiegelman was awarded a special Pulitzer Prize for his work. In addition to the Pulitzer, he has received several other awards, including a Guggenheim fellowship, an Eisner Award (for "Best Graphic Album"), and a nomination for the National Book Critics Circle Award. In 2005, he was named one of the 100 Most Influential People by *Time* magazine.

Art Spiegelman lives in New York City with his wife and two children, Nadja and Dashiell. Recent works include *Little Lit*, a series of comics for children, and *In the Shadow of No Towers*, an autobiographical account of the September 11th attacks and aftermath, told as a graphic novel. His work has been published in the *New York Times*, *Playboy*, *The Village Voice*, and the *New Yorker*. He received an honorary doctorate from Binghamton University in 1995.

About MAUS

Art Spiegelman's *Maus* is the most unlikely of creations: a comic book about the Holocaust. Yet when the first volume of *Maus* was published in 1987, it met with enormous critical and commercial success, and to this day it is widely considered to be among the best and most powerful of a long list of Holocaust–inspired works. When the second volume was published in 1991, the completed work was awarded a special Pulitzer Prize for Letters, an almost unprecedented honor for a medium usually reserved for super heroes and the Sunday comics (though to be fair, the creators of Doonesbury and Bloom County, popular Sunday comics, have also won Pulitzers for their work).

In *Maus*, the different races and nationalities within the story are portrayed as different kinds of animals. Jews, for example, are portrayed as mice, while the Germans are depicted as cats. A precursor to *Maus* was first published in an underground comic magazine called *Funny Animals* in 1972. The piece was only three pages long, but many of the same elements were there, including the focus on his father, Vladek Spiegelman, and the decision to portray Jews as mice. The artwork was, however, more overtly comical and cartoonish. Spiegelman continued to work on his creation, and in 1980, when he co–founded the underground comic magazine *Raw*, he began publishing *Maus* as a serial graphic novel, which appeared in six installments between 1981 and 1986. These installments were colleted and published as *Maus I: My Father Bleeds History* in 1987. The publication of *Maus II: And Here My Troubles Began*, followed a similar route, appearing as a serial in *Raw* before being published in full in 1992.

Maus consists of two primary narratives of equal importance. The first major narrative is directed by Art's father, Vladek Spiegelman, who offers the story of his experiences in the Holocaust, as told to his son through a series of interviews. This narrative begins in pre–war Poland and tracks his life over a period of approximately ten years, from his marriage to his wife, Anja, in 1937, through his experiences in Auschwitz, and to his eventual immigration to Sweden after the war. The second major narrative focuses on Art's complex and conflicted relationship with his father between 1978 and 1982, while he interviews the old man about his Holocaust experiences.

In addition to these primary narratives, there are also two "minor" narratives that appear only briefly within the story. The first of these is a short comic that Art Spiegelman originally published in 1972, which details the story of Art's mother's suicide in 1968. The comic is eventually discovered by Vladek and reprinted in full in the middle of the first volume of *Maus*. The second minor narrative occurs at the beginning of the second chapter of *Maus II* and takes place in 1987, shortly after the publication of *Maus I*. It is a deeply personal and self–reflective narrative revealing the conflicting emotions of the author with regards to his father and the publication of *Maus*.

Though *Maus* is a comic book, its impact and complexity are far greater than most works of this medium. The story explores the nature of guilt, and the narrative serves as a meditation on the effects of a major historical event – in this case the traumatic events of the Holocaust – on the lives of people who were born after it ended. With its complex themes and structure and unconventional medium of a graphic novel, *Maus* almost defies description. Equal parts fiction, biography, autobiography, and history, it is in many ways a book that rises above genre to become something completely unique, and it is an amazing and lasting story that is destined to become a classic.

Character List

Art Spiegelman

Art Spiegelman is the author and narrator of *Maus*, and also one of the story's main characters. Born in Stockholm after the Holocaust, he is the only surviving child of Vladek and Anja Spiegelman. His brother, Richieu, died as a child during the war, and his mother committed suicide in 1968 when he was twenty years old. He has a history of mental illness and is married to Francoise, a French woman who converted to Judaism upon their engagement. *Maus* centers around two primary narratives: Vladek's experiences as a Jew in World War II Poland, and Art's relationship with his aging father. This second narrative follows a period of time in Art's life beginning around 1978 and ending sometime shortly before Vladek's death in 1982.

When the story opens, Art lives in New York and does not see his father very often, though he lives only a short distance away in Queens. But as Art begins to draw this story about Vladek's Holocaust experiences, he begins to visit his father more and more frequently. Their relationship is strained, as Vladek's gruff demeanor and unwillingness to spend money routinely infuriate his son. Art is filled with complex feelings towards his father ranging from admiration for his survival in Auschwitz, to frustration towards his aggravating tendencies, and guilt for his own neglect of a father who has lived through so many difficult times.

Art also has complex emotions towards the Holocaust. Though he did not live through it personally, he feels that he is constantly affected by it. His father's personality was largely formed from his experiences in Auschwitz, and this personality in turn directly affected the way in which Art was raised. Art is consumed by varied feelings of guilt, especially regarding the fact that his life has been so much easier than his parents'. He sometimes wishes that he had been in Auschwitz, so that he would know what they went through.

Vladek Spiegelman

Vladek is Art Spiegelman's father. He grew up in pre–war Poland, and much of *Maus* traces his experiences in the Holocaust, as told in his own words to his son. As the story opens in 1978, he is married to his second wife, Mala. The couple does not get along, and they are briefly separated in *Maus*'s second volume. Mala is furious about the fact that he does not give her any money, even for things that she needs. Vladek, on the other hand, views Mala with a suspicion that borders on spite, and is constantly afraid that she is trying to steal the money that he has spent a lifetime saving.

Vladek marries Art's mother, Anja, in Poland in 1937, only two years before the Nazi invasion. Anja's father is a wealthy manufacturer, and he provides Vladek with his own textile factory upon their marriage. Shortly thereafter, they have their first child, a boy named Richieu, who will die a few years later as a victim of the Holocaust. Vladek and Anja ultimately survive the war, and afterwards they move to Sweden for two years before settling in America. While living in Stockholm, they have their second child, Art. Anja kills herself in 1968, and Vladek mourns her until his death in 1982.

Vladek's personality is largely dominated by his Holocaust experiences. During the Holocaust, he exhibited a spectacular resourcefulness, work ethic, and presence of mind that often enabled him to secure food, shelter, and safety for himself and his family. He was a shrewd businessman, and in the most troubling times he saved everything of use. In 1978, he still saves everything and tries to exchange those things that he no longer needs. Once so resourceful and competent, he is still constantly working on small projects, some of which he is incapable of completing. His last words of the story, in which he accidentally calls Art by the name of his son who died in the war, provide a final testament to the continuing relevance of the Holocaust in Vladek's life.

Anja Spiegelman

Anja is Art's mother and Vladek's first wife. The couple meets in Poland while Vladek is in a long–term relationship with another woman, Lucia Greenberg. They marry in 1937. Shortly after, they have their first child, a boy named Richieu, who will die during the war. Always an anxious woman, she suffers an acute depression shortly after the birth of her son and spends three months recovering in a sanitarium. Her father is a wealthy manufacturer who provides Vladek with his own textile factory, and the two live in comfort for a short while, until the German invasion in 1939. She survives the Holocaust with her husband, and they immigrate to the United States a few years after the war.

Anja commits suicide in 1968, leaving both Art and Vladek in emotional turmoil. Art's last memory of his mother is recorded in a comic called "Prisoner on the Hell Planet," in which she enters Art's room and asks him if he still loves her. His response, a terse and dismissive "sure," haunts him for years.

Richieu Spiegelman

Richieu is Vladek and Anja's first child, born in Poland in 1937. In 1943, Vladek and Anja send him to live under the protection of Uncle Persis, where they think he will be safer. Richieu travels with Anja's sister, Tosha; Tosha's daughter, Bibbi; and Vladek's niece, Lonia. But soon after, Zawiercie is liquidated by the Nazis. Rather than be taken to the gas chamber, Tosha poisons herself and the children under her care, including Richieu. After his death, Vladek and Anja keep a photograph of their first child hanging on the wall of their bedroom, and Art comes to feel a sense of sibling rivalry with his "ghost brother."

Mala Spiegelman

Mala is Vladek's second wife, and a friend of his family from before the war. The couple does not get along. Mala is consumed with frustration towards Vladek's inability to part with money, while Vladek views his wife with considerable distrust and accuses her of trying to steal his money. Fed up with her husband, Mala eventually leaves him and moves to Florida, though they are later reunited against her better judgment. Like Vladek, she is a Holocaust survivor.

Francoise

Art's wife. She is French and converted to Judaism in preparation for their marriage to please Vladek. She is intelligent, kind, and opinionated, and their relationship is strong. She plays a relatively minor role in the story, serving mostly as a means for Art to discuss his relationship with his father and the Holocaust.

Mr. Zylberberg

Anja's father. Before the war, he is a wealthy manufacturer who owns a hosiery factory. When Vladek and Anja are married, he provides Vladek with a factory of his own. He survives with his family in German–occupied Poland, until the family is captured and sent to await transport to Auschwitz. By bribing his cousin, Haskel, Vladek is able to arrange for the release of himself and Anja. Though Haskel also accepts payment for the release of Anja's parents, he is ultimately unwilling to help them, and the two eventually die in Auschwitz.

Orbach

A friend of Vladek's family in Poland. When Vladek is a prisoner of war, Orbach claims him as a cousin, so that Vladek is released into his custody and eventually returns home to Sosnowiec.

Vladek's father

Vladek's father is a tough and deeply religious man. His wife dies of cancer before the worst of the Holocaust. Before the war, Vladek's father intentionally starves his son so that he will be declared unfit for the army. Later, the Nazi grip tightens, and all Jews are made to register in a nearby stadium. Those who are fit to work are sent to one side, while the elderly and women with many children are sent to their deaths at the concentration camps. By registering at a table manned by his cousin, Mordecai, Vladek's father is spared. Before he leaves the stadium, however, he sees his daughter, Fela (Vladek's sister) and her four small children standing with those destined for Auschwitz. He crosses over to be with her, and all die in the camps.

Uncle Herman

Anja's brother. Along with his wife, Hela, he is visiting the New York World's Fair when the war begins, and they remain in the United States to escape the horrors abroad. He has a son of about 15 years, Lolek, and a young daughter, Lonia. Lolek is sent to Auschwitz but survives, while Lonia is poisoned by Anja's sister, Tosha, rather than be sent to the gas chambers.

Tosha

Tosha is Anja's older sister. At the beginning of the German occupation of Poland, she lives with Anja's family in her father's house, along with her husband, Wolfe, and their small daughter, Bibbi. As the situation deteriorates Uncle Persis offers to keep her safely in nearby Zawiercie ghetto, where he is a prominent member of the Jewish Council. She agrees, and leaves with Wolfe, Bibbi, and Vladek's son Richieu. Soon, though, the Germans slaughter the Jewish Council and begin to evacuate the Jews of Zawiercie to the camps. Rather than be sent to the gas chambers, Tosha poisons herself, her daughter, Herman's daughter Lonia, and Vladek's son Richieu.

Mr. Ilzecki

A former customer of Vladek's from before the war. The two meet again after the German occupation and begin conducting business on the Sosnowiec black market. Mr. Ilzecki has a son about the same age as Vladek's, and he offers to send Richieu along with his own son to a Polish friend to hide until things get better. Vladek thinks this is a good idea, but Anja refuses. Mr. Ilzecki's son will survive the war; Richieu will not. Mr. Ilzecki himself dies in the Holocaust.

Nahum Cohn

A friend and business partner of Vladek's during his black market days in Sosnowiec. Nahum is arrested along with his son for selling goods without coupons. The Nazis decide to make an example of them and they are hanged in a well–know black market center and left there for a full week.

Anja's Grandparents

During the initial period of the German occupation, they live in Anja's father's house with the rest of the family. Later, they are told to relocate to a "community better prepared to take care of the elderly." The family hides them for over a month, until the authorities arrest Anja's father and threaten to arrest more of his family if the grandparents are not given over to the Germans. Anja's grandparents are taken away to Auschwitz, where they are killed.

Lolek

Vladek's nephew and Uncle Herman's son. Lolek lives with Anja's family for much of the initial German occupation, first at Anja's father's house and then in the Srodula ghetto. When the situation deteriorates and Vladek makes preparations to hide in a shelter until the Nazis have evacuated the town, Lolek tells his uncle that he is tired of hiding, and he is soon transported to Auschwitz.

He survives the camps and eventually becomes a college professor.

Haskel Spiegelman

Haskel is Vladek's cousin, and chief of the Jewish Police in the Srodula ghetto. He is the brother of Miloch and Pesach. He is what Vladek calls a kombinacya, or "schemer." While he is a rather unsavory character, he is a good person to know in the ghetto. When Vladek's family is discovered in the "chandelier" bunker and sent to a compound to wait for transport to Auschwitz, Haskel arranges for Vladek, Anja, and Lolek to be released in exchange for valuables. He also accepts valuables for assistance in releasing Anja's parents, but ultimately refuses to help them. Upon their release, he arranges for them to work at a shoe repair shop resoling German boots. Haskel ultimately survives the war, and Vladek sends him packages for some time afterwards.

Miloch Spiegelman

Miloch is Vladek's cousin, and brother to Haskel and Pesach. He is Vladek's supervisor at the shoe repair shop in the Srodula ghetto, and an honorable man compared to the scheming Haskel. When the Germans make plans to eliminate all Jews in the ghetto, he prepares a hidden shelter behind a pile of shoes at the shop, where Vladek, Anja, and 15 other people hide for days. After the Germans evacuate the ghetto, Miloch hides at his old house in Sosnowiec, hidden by his former maid in the garbage pile with his wife and small child. When Vladek attempts to flee to Hungary, Miloch and his family hide with Mrs. Motonowa, with whom they safely survive the war.

Pesach Spiegelman

Pesach is Vladek's cousin, and brother to Miloch and Pesach. Like Haskel, he is a schemer and a rather unsavory character. His most significant involvement centers on a scheme to sell cake to the inhabitants of the ghetto. He makes a fortune, but everyone who eats it becomes sick – the cake was accidentally made with laundry soap in addition to flour. When the Germans liquidate the Srodula ghetto, he hides with Vladek and Miloch in the shelter behind the pile of shoes. Eventually, though, he becomes tired of waiting and bribes some German guards to look the other way as he escapes. He is betrayed and killed by the same guards.

Mr. Lukowski

The janitor at Anja's father's house. When Vladek and Anja escape from the Srodula ghetto, they knock on his door and he allows them to stay in a shed behind his house. They eventually leave to hide at Mrs. Kawka's farm.

Mrs. Kawka

Mrs. Kawka is the owner of a small farm on the outskirts of Sosnowiec, and for a price she allows Vladek and Anja to hide in her barn. She is outwardly gruff but also has a kinder side. They eventually leave to hide at Mrs. Motonowa's house. Mrs. Kawka is the person who tells Vladek about the smugglers who can take him to Hungary.

Mrs. Motonowa

Vladek befriends Mrs. Motonowa at the Sosnowiec black market after the liquidation of Srodula, and she offers to hide him and Anja at her farm, with her seven–year–old son. She is a kind woman, and the house is comfortable, except for a ten–day period in which Mrs. Motonowa's husband returns home from Germany on vacation, and they are forced to stay in the basement. One evening, she is searched by the Gestapo in the black market, and she becomes worried that they will return to search her house. Terrified, she forces the Spiegelmans to leave. A few days later, however, Vladek sees her again at the black market. She feels terrible about kicking them out, and the Spiegelmans return to live with her again. After Vladek and Anja attempt to escape to Hungary, she shelters Miloch and his family for the remainder of the war.

Mandelbaum

Before the war, Mandelbaum owned a pastry store in Sosnowiec where Vladek and Anja often shopped. Vladek sees him again while meeting with the smugglers who will take him to Hungary. His cousin, Abraham, is also with them. When they are betrayed by the smugglers, Mandelbaum is sent to Auschwitz with Vladek. He has a difficult time at the camp and ultimately dies there.

Abraham

Abraham is Mandelbaum's cousin. He agrees to accompany the smugglers, and promises to write Mandelbaum and Vladek if he arrives safely in Hungary. He is betrayed, however, and forced at gunpoint to write the letter anyway. Though Vladek is not certain, he thinks that Abraham is ultimately killed at Auschwitz.

The Karps

The Karps are Vladek's neighbors at his Catskills bungalow. When Art visits his father there, they take him aside and tell him that Vladek cannot possibly take care of himself.

Vladek's Kapo

A "kapo" is a Polish supervisor at a concentration camp. Soon after Vladek arrives at Auschwitz, Vladek's kapo asks the Jews in the barracks if anyone there can speak English. Vladek volunteers, and the kapo takes him on as a tutor. He keeps Vladek safe in the quarantine block for as long as he can, and he provides him with extra food and clothing. Ultimately, Vladek must start working, and the kapo helps Vladek find work as a tinsmith, since skilled laborers get better treatment.

Pavel

Pavel is Art's psychiatrist. Like Art's father, Pavel is a survivor of the Holocaust. Art sees him once a week, and the sessions always seem to make him feel better.

Yidl

Yidl is Vladek's boss at the tin shop in Auschwitz. He is Communist and Jewish, and he despises Vladek for having owned a factory before the war and for not knowing how to work with tin. Vladek is terrified that Yidl will report him, so he arranges to give him frequent gifts of food.

Mancie

Mancie is a female Hungarian Jew at Birkenau with Anja, and has higher status as a result of an affair with S.S. guard. She acts as a go–between for Vladek and his wife, carrying notes and food.

The Frenchman

After Vladek is transferred from Auschwitz to Dachau, he befriends a Frenchman with whom he converses in English. Because he is not Jewish, the Frenchman is able to receive packages of food through the Red Cross, which he shares with Vladek, probably saving his life.

Shivek

A friend of Vladek's from before the war, they meet again upon their release from the concentration camps. Together, they escape the remaining German patrols and eventually find their way to an American base camp, and then to a displaced persons camp. Afterwards, they travel together to Shivek's brother's house in Hannover. They then begin heading towards Poland, but are separated. Shivek returns to Hannover, while Vladek continues on to Sosnowiec.

The Gypsy

After being released from the concentration camps, Anja is able to return to Sosnowiec before Vladek. Though she knows it is foolish, she visits a gypsy fortuneteller to find news of her husband. The gypsy looks into her crystal ball and sees the death of everyone in her family, including her father, mother, and child. But she sees that her husband is still alive, and together they will find a new life in another part of the world, with a new little boy.

Major Themes

Familial Guilt

While on its surface *Maus* is the story of Vladek Spiegelman's experiences in the Holocaust, it is also much more. In many ways, the relationship between Vladek and his son is the central narrative in the book, and this narrative deals extensively with feelings of guilt. Of particular relevance in *Maus* is the guilt that is associated with the members of one's family. The primary types of familial guilt can be divided into three separate categories: 1) Art's feelings of guilt over not being a good son; 2) Art's feelings of guilt over the death of his mother; and 3) Art's feelings of guilt regarding the publication of *Maus*.

The simplest form of guilt in *Maus* is Art's guilt over the fact that he thinks he has not been a good son to his father. Right from the first panel of Book I, we are told that the two of them do not get along particularly well, and that they do not see each other often, though they live fairly close by. Art is always on edge around his father, and when they speak it feels as if an argument could break out at any moment. Indeed, arguments often do break out over, for example, Art's dropping cigarette ash on the carpet, or Vladek's revelation that he has burned Anja's diaries from the war. Vladek often asks his son for help with errands around the house, and Art is always loath to comply. One of the most prominent examples of this situation occurs at the beginning of Chapter 5 of Book I, in which Vladek awakens his son early in the morning to ask for help fixing a drain on his roof. Art refuses, later telling his wife that he would rather feel guilty than travel to Queens to help his father. A few weeks later, during Art's next visit to his father, this guilt is painfully obvious, as he immediately asks his father if he needs help with any chores.

Art's feelings of guilt over the death of his mother are also relatively straightforward. As told in the brief "Prisoner on the Hell Planet" interlude in Chapter 5 of Book I, Art feels responsible for his mother's suicide, believing it to be a product of his own neglect. His last memory of his mother – in which she asks him if he still loves her, and he responds with a cold and dismissive "sure" – is a painful reminder of this disregard. Though this particular form of guilt does not play a major role in the story, it is noteworthy in that Art feels somewhat similar feelings of guilt towards his father, who is still alive.

After the first volume of *Maus* is published in 1986, four years after his father's death in 1982, Art is still consumed with guilt. The publication of *Maus* has not alleviated these feelings, and in some ways it has made them worse. "My father's ghost still hangs over me," Art says before walking to his appointment with Pavel. Pavel suggests that Art may be feeling remorse for portraying Vladek unfavorably. Pavel also suggests, in an interesting reversal, that perhaps Vladek himself felt guilty for having survived the Holocaust. This form of guilt, "survivor's guilt," is detailed in the next section.

Survivor's Guilt

The second form of guilt found in the pages of *Maus* is more thematically complex. This guilt, called "survivor's guilt," is the product of both Vladek and Art's relationships with the Holocaust. Much of *Maus* revolves around this relationship between past and present, and the effects of past events on the lives of those who did not experience them (see below). In the cases of both men, this relationship often manifests itself as guilt.

Though Art was born in Sweden after the end of World War II, both of his parents were survivors of the Holocaust, and the event has affected him deeply. In Chapter One of Book II, as Art and Francoise are driving to the Catskills, Art reflects on this in detail, and Art's relationship with the past is revealed to predominantly take the form of guilt: "Somehow, I wish I had been in Auschwitz with my parents so I could really know what they lived through! I guess it's some form of guilt about having had an easier life than they did."

Vladek, too, appears to feel a deep sense of guilt about having survived the Holocaust. As Art's guilt persists through the late 1980s, five years after the death of his father, he visits his psychiatrist, Pavel, and the two discuss the nature of guilt and what it means to be a Holocaust "survivor." Vladek's survival in the Holocaust was not the consequence of any particular skill, but the result of luck, both good and bad. Pavel turns the idea of guilt on its head by suggesting that Vladek himself actually felt a strong sense of guilt for having survived the Holocaust while so many of his friends and family did not. And perhaps in response, Vladek took this guilt out on Art, the "real survivor," as Pavel calls him. In essence, Vladek's guilt may have been passed down to his son, establishing the foundation for the volumes of guilt that Art now feels towards his family and its history.

Past and Present

Maus consists of two primary narratives: one that takes place in World War II Poland, and the other that takes place in late 1970s/early 1980s New York. The relationship between these two narratives – and more generally between the past and present – is a central theme of the story. The events of the Holocaust continue to influence the life of Vladek, a Holocaust survivor, and reverberate through future generations, ultimately affecting his son, Art.

Many of Vladek's peculiar personality traits can be linked to his experiences in the Holocaust. In 1978, Vladek is stubborn, irritable, and almost comically stingy with his money. His relationship with his second wife, Mala, is strained and seemingly devoid of love. Prior to World War II, however, he exhibits none of these characteristics. He is kind, wealthy, and uncommonly resourceful, and his marriage to Anja is filled with compassion and intimacy. His experiences in the Holocaust undoubtedly played a role in these dramatic personality changes.

Once relatively wealthy, Vladek's survival in German–occupied Poland depended on his ability to hoard and save even the smallest of items, such as the paper wrapper from a piece of cheese, or the cigarettes from his weekly rations. These small items took on enormous importance to Vladek, and even many years later, he feels unable to throw anything away. His stubbornness in 1978 can be explained by the fact that he survived the Holocaust largely because he possessed a remarkable intelligence and resourcefulness that enabled him to acquire the necessary food, supplies, shelter, and protection. Now he is much older, but he still thinks of himself as the same young man who could do everything on his own. He still wants to act accordingly, going to such extremes as climbing onto the roof to fix a leaky drain. Still, as Art notes on a few separate occasions, the Holocaust cannot explain everything about his father: "I used to think the war made him this way," Art reflects to Mala, in Chapter Six of Book I, to which she responds that "all our friends went through the camps; nobody is like him!" Vladek has clearly never fully recovered from the horrors of the Holocaust. This fact is poignantly illustrated by his final words of the story, when he mistakenly calls Art by the name of his first child, who died during the war.

Though Art was born in Sweden after the war and did not experience the Holocaust firsthand, his life has also been deeply affected by these unspeakable events. To begin with, Art is directly affected by secondary "aftershocks" of the Holocaust, in that Vladek's personality and parenting style were clearly influenced by these events, and Art's personality and lifestyle choices were in turn clearly guided by his father's personality and parenting style. Art describes a specific instance of this transmission to his wife:

> [Vladek] loved showing off how handy he was… and proving that anything I did was all wrong. He made me completely neurotic about fixing stuff…One reason I became an artist was…it was an area where I wouldn't have to compete with him.

Art is also affected by the past in less direct ways. To begin with, he feels almost completely consumed by the horrible specter of the Holocaust. As a child, he sometimes fantasized that the showers in his house would spew gas instead of water, and he would often ask himself which parent he would save if he could have only saved one from Auschwitz (he usually picked his mother). In many ways, he feels guilty about the fact that his parents were forced to live through Auschwitz, whereas he was born after it ended, into a far more comfortable and easy life.

The relationships between past and present are often illustrated graphically within the context of the story. The most vivid representation of this concept occurs at the beginning of Chapter Two of Book II, in which Art is sitting at his drawing board above a sprawling pile of dead and emaciated Jewish mice.

Survival

The primary motivation amongst Jews in the Holocaust is survival. Vladek sums up the process succinctly while consoling his wife after the death of his first son, Richieu: "to die, it's easy…but you have to struggle for life." Vladek's experiences in the Holocaust represent a constant struggle to survive, first as his factory and income are taken away, then as the Jews are sent into the ghettos, and ultimately in the nightmare of Auschwitz. And as the struggle intensifies, the will to survive begins to break the strong bonds of family, friendship, and a common Jewish identity.

In the initial stages of German occupation, these measures are relatively small – buying food on the black market, for example – and strengthened by strong family ties, a unified Jewish identity, and even altruism. When Vladek arrives home from the prisoner of war camp, for example, an old business acquaintance, Mr. Ilzecki, helps him earn money and acquire the proper work papers that will allow him to walk the streets in relative safety. As the situation continues to deteriorate, however, Vladek, his family, and his friends are forced to resort to increasingly extreme measures in order to survive. Here, the bonds of Jewish identity begin to break under the pressing instinct to survive. The first sign of this comes in the form of Jews serving on a Jewish Police force, like the ones who came to Vladek's apartment to escort his wife's grandparents to the concentration camps. According to Vladek, these Jews thought that by helping the Nazis in taking some of the Jews, perhaps they could help save others – and of course they could also save themselves. Soon after, the bonds of family also begin to break, as illustrated by Vladek's cousin Haskel's refusal to save them from transport to Auschwitz without some form of payment. Though Haskel eventually does help Vladek and Anja escape, he ultimately decides not to help Anja's parents, and they are sent off to their deaths.

The bond between Vladek and Anja remains solid throughout most of the story, as they first hide together in the barns and back rooms of Sosnowiec and are ultimately sent to neighboring concentration camps. In the camps, Vladek and Anja are both preoccupied with their own survival, but Vladek is also able to help his wife by giving her extra food and emotional support. Soon, though, the Russians advance upon Auschwitz and Birkenau, and the couple is unavoidably separated. Vladek is hurried on a long, forced march through snow–covered woods to packed railway cars where there is no food or water for days. In telling this story to his son, Vladek does not mention Anja again until right before their eventual reunification in Sosnowiec. Unable to help those around him, and unable to help his wife, he is left only with his own stubborn will to survive.

Luck

The importance of luck is closely related to discussions of survival and guilt (see above). Vladek is blessed with many skills and qualities – including the ability to speak multiple languages – that provide him with opportunities to survive within the confines of Auschwitz. Ultimately, however, Vladek's survival and the survival of all other Holocaust survivors hinges upon luck. On countless occasions throughout Vladek's Holocaust ordeals, his life is spared only by the narrowest of margins: the near–miss bullet at the prisoner–of–war camp in Lublin; the run–in with the Gestapo while carrying ten kilograms of illegal sugar; the night Mrs. Motonowa forces him and Anja out of her house; the case of typhus at Dachau; and many, many other incidents. No matter how resourceful Vladek is, no matter how many languages he knows or jobs he can perform, he cannot ultimately save himself from the horrors of the Holocaust. Rather, the matter of his life and death ultimately depends upon a long line of chance outcomes, most of which happen to fall his way. The rest of his family, including his parents and five siblings, are not so lucky. Pavel, Art's psychiatrist, suggests that this idea may have contributed to a strong sense of guilt in Vladek for having survived the Holocaust while so many of his friends and family did not.

Race and Class

Unsurprisingly, given the subject matter, issues of race and class figure heavily in the plot, themes, and structure of *Maus*. At the most basic level, issues of race play themselves out on the grand scale of the Holocaust, a terrible culmination of senseless racism that is drawn and described in all its brutality and efficiency. But *Maus* also deals with these issues in other, more subtle ways, through the use of different animal faces to portray different races.

In *Maus*, Jews are portrayed as mice, while Germans are portrayed as cats. The metaphor of Jews as mice is taken directly from Nazi propaganda, which portrayed the Jews as a kind of vermin to be exterminated. The cat/mouse relationship is also an apt metaphor for the relationship between the Nazis and Jews: the Nazis toyed with the Jews before ultimately killing them.

The decision to portray different races as different kinds of animals has been criticized as over–simplistic and for promoting ethnic stereotypes. Beneath the simple metaphor, however, is an earnest attempt to illustrate the unyielding stratification by class and race that was very much a part of life in World War II–era Poland. Within the pages of Vladek's story, the Jews are rarely seen socializing with the non–Jewish Poles, except in cases where the Poles serve as janitors, governesses, or other household assistants. The idea of stratification and classification is best illustrated by the man in the concentration camp who claims that he is German, not Jewish, and who is ultimately taken aside and killed. When Art asks his father whether the man was really a German, Vladek replies, "who knows…it was German prisoners in there also…But for the Germans this guy was Jewish." There were no shades of gray within the German system of racial classification. Indeed, this middle ground is so rare within the pages of *Maus* that the only instance of mixed marriage (Shivek's brother, who married a German woman) comes as quite a shock, especially when we see their children, who are drawn as cat/mouse hybrids.

This, however, is not the only form of racism that exists within the pages of *Maus*. One of the most interesting aspects of the story is the fact that Vladek, who survived the horrors of the Holocaust, is himself a racist. When Francoise picks up an African–American hitchhiker on their way back from the grocery store, Vladek can hardly contain his anger that she has let a "shvartser" into the car and spends the whole ride home watching his groceries to make sure they aren't stolen. This episode serves as a reminder that the racism of the Holocaust survives in other forms to this day.

Just as the animal metaphor is an attempt to explain an existing social stratification, other aspects of the story seem to suggest that this stratification is a manufactured illusion. This is most clearly illustrated in opening pages of Chapter Two of Book II, which take place after the publication of the first book of *Maus*. In this narrative, Art Spiegelman is clearly having doubts about the animal metaphors that form the backbone of the story. Here, people are still characterized by animals based on race, but these characterizations are now clearly only masks that have been tied to their heads with a bit of string. Thus the idea of race is only an artifice, Spiegelman suggests, and underneath the masks we are all essentially the same.

Glossary of Terms

Absolution

Forgiveness of an offense; a setting free from guilt or sin

Abundant

Amply supplied

Anti–Semitism

A prejudice against Jews

Aryan

A term used by the Nazis to signify the "master race" of people of northern European descent

Barrack

A building or set of buildings used especially for lodging soldiers in garrison

Bungalow

A small house or cottage, usually containing a single story

Cataract

A clouding of the lens of the eye or the surrounding transparent membrane that obstructs the passage of light

Claustrophobic

Having a fear or dread of closed spaces

Conjugate

To list the forms of a verb

Convalesce

To recover health and strength gradually after a sickness or weakness

Crematorium

An establishment containing a furnace for burning (usually bodies)

Dowry

The money, goods, or estate that a woman brings to her husband in marriage

Gefilte Fish

A ground, deboned fish recipe using a variety of kosher fish meat

Gestapo

The official secret police of Nazi Germany

Ghetto

A quarter of a city in which members of a minority group live especially because of social, legal, or economic pressure

Governess

A woman who cares for and supervises a child, especially in a private household

Marks

German currency

Meshuga

Yiddish word for "crazy" or "foolish"

Miserly

Stingy, cautious with money

Munitions

Ammunition, armaments

Naugahyde

A synthetic leather made from plastic

Nitrostat

Medicine taken for relief of angina, chest pains caused by a lack of blood flow to the heart muscle

Notary

An officer who can administer oaths and statutory declarations, witness and authenticate documents, and perform certain other official acts

Nu

A Yiddish word roughly equivalent to "so?" or "well?"

Oy Gevalt

A Yiddish expression of exasperation

Pogrom

An organized massacre of helpless people, especially of Jews

Pragmatic

Practical, as opposed to idealistic

Presumptuous

Overconfident, audacious, arrogant

Sanitarium

An institution for rest and recuperation

Schnell

A German word meaning "faster"

Sheik

An Arab chief; a man held to be irresistibly attractive to romantic young women

Shrink

A slang term for a psychiatrist

Shvartser

A Yiddish word for a black or African–American man

Textile

A woven or knit cloth; a fiber, filament, or yarn used in making cloth

Tuchus

A Yiddish word meaning "rear end"

Valentino, Rudolph

A movie star in the 1920s, one of the first great Hollywood sex symbols

Valise

A suitcase

Wehrmacht

A German word for the Nazi armed forces

Yiddish

A language written in Hebrew and spoken by Jews

Zloty

A unit of Polish currency

Short Summary

Note: *Maus* jumps back and forth often between the past and the present. To facilitate these transitions in this summary, the Holocaust narrative is written in normal font, while all other narratives are written in italics.

Book I: My Father Bleeds History

As the book opens, it is 1978, and Art Spiegelman arrives in Rego Park, NY, to dine with his father, Vladek, a Holocaust survivor. It is immediately apparent that the two men are not particularly close. Art's mother, Anja, killed herself in 1968, and Vladek is now remarried to a woman named Mala, herself a survivor. The couple does not get along, and there does not appear to be much love in their relationship. Vladek, constantly fearful that Mala will steal his money, is intensely stingy and treats his wife like little more than a maid. After dinner, Art tells his father that he wants to draw a book about his experiences in the Holocaust, and Vladek starts to tell his son the story of how he met Anja.

It is 1936. Vladek is living in Czestochowa, Poland, and has been dating a girl named Lucia Greenberg for several years. One day he travels to Sosnowiec and is introduced to Anja, the intelligent daughter of a wealthy manufacturer. They are married in 1937, and Anja's father gives Vladek part–ownership in his profitable business. Anja gives birth to the couple's first child, Richieu, soon after the marriage. After the birth, Anja becomes consumed with depression, and Vladek takes her to a sanitarium for the next three months. When they return, Vladek is drafted into the Polish army and sent west to guard the border in anticipation of a German attack.

As the Germans advance, Vladek manages to kill one soldier before he is captured and taken to a prisoner of war camp. One night, Vladek dreams of his grandfather, who tells him that he will be released during the Jewish week of Parshas Truma. Three months later, it is Parshas Truma, and Vladek is indeed released. When he returns to Sosnowiec, there are twelve people living in Anja's father's house. The family's business has been taken over by the Germans, and they are living off of their savings. Vladek meets an old customer, Mr. Ilzecki, and the two begin a dangerous business of black market dealings.

In 1942, the Jews are forced to move to a separate part of town. Soon after, Anja's grandparents are told to report for transport to a new community for the elderly. The family hides them, but soon they are taken away to Auschwitz. Not long after, all remaining Jews are told to report to a nearby stadium for "registration." Here, the elderly, families with many children, and people without work cards are sent to the left, while everyone else is taken to the right. Those on the left are sent to their deaths at Auschwitz. Vladek's father is sent to the right, but when he sees his daughter alone with her four children on the left, he crosses over to be with her. None survive the war.

Art speaks briefly with Mala about her own Holocaust experiences before going to the living room to look for his mother's diaries, in which Vladek said she had recorded all her experiences during the war. He cannot find them.

A few days later, Mala calls Art early in the morning in hysterics. Vladek, it seems, climbed on top of the roof in an attempt to fix a leaky drain and then climbed back down because he felt dizzy. Art does not want to help, and Vladek finally arranges for his neighbor to help him. A week later, Art visits his father, clearly feeling guilty. Vladek is upset, having found a comic Art had drawn years ago about the death of Anja, titled "Prisoner on the Hell Planet: A Case Study." In the comic, Vladek arrives home in 1968 to see his wife dead in the bathtub. Art has just arrived home from a stretch in a state mental institution, and he feels responsible for his mother's suicide due to neglect and a lack of affection.

In 1943, all Jews are forced into a ghetto in the nearby town of Srodula. Uncle Persis, chief of the Jewish council in the nearby ghetto of Zawiercie, tells Vladek that he can keep Richieu in safety until things calm down. Vladek and Anja agree, and Richieu is sent there with Anja's sister, Tosha. Soon afterwards the Zawiercie ghetto is liquidated by the Nazis. Rather than be sent to the Auschwitz, Tosha poisons herself, her daughter, and Richieu.

In Srodula, Vladek constructs a series of bunkers in which the family can hide during the Nazi raids, but they are eventually captured and sent to a compound to await transport to Auschwitz. By bribing his cousin, Haskel, chief of the Jewish Police, Vladek is able to arrange for the release of himself and his wife, but Anja's parents are sent to Auschwitz. Miloch and Pesach, Haskel's brothers, build a bunker behind a pile of shoes in the factory where Vladek and Anja hide for many days without food, until the ghetto is finally evacuated. Unsure of where to go, Anja and Vladek walk back to Sosnowiec.

On his next visit, Art finds Mala crying at the kitchen table. She is miserable in her marriage and thinks Vladek is both cheap and insensitive. Vladek walks into the room, and the two begin to argue over money. Mala leaves in a huff.

Anja and Vladek return to Sosnowiec. They knock on the door of her father's old janitor, who hides them in his shed. They soon move to a safer place – a farm outside the city owned by a Mrs. Kawka. But it is getting cold, and they need a warmer place to live. Vladek befriends a kindly black market grocer named Mrs. Motonowa, who offers her home to the Spiegelmans. The arrangement is comfortable, but one day Mrs. Motonowa is searched by the Gestapo at the market and returns home in a panic, kicking them out of the house. They live on the streets for the night and eventually return to Mrs. Kawka's, who tells them of smugglers who will take them to safety in Hungary.

A few days later, Mrs. Motonowa apologizes and they hide with her again. But Vladek does not feel safe, and he arranges to meet with the smugglers. An old acquaintance, Mandelbaum, is also at the meeting with his nephew, Abraham. Abraham agrees to travel first and write to them if he arrives safely in Hungary. A few days later, they receive a letter from Abraham and board a train with the smugglers, but they are arrested by the Gestapo and sent to the concentration camps.

Back in Rego Park, Vladek tells Art that he burned his wife's diaries shortly after her death in an attempt to ease his own pain. Art is furious and calls his father a murderer.

Book II: And Here My Troubles Began

Vladek leaves a message saying he has just had a heart attack. When Art calls the number his father left, he learns that Vladek is healthy and staying in a bungalow in the Catskills. He left the message, it appears, to ensure that his son would call him back. Mala has left him, and Art and Francoise immediately depart for the Catskills. On the drive, Art tells Francoise about his complex feelings about the Holocaust, including the guilt he feels for having had an easier life than his parents.

Vladek arrives at Auschwitz with Mandelbaum. All around, there is a terrible smell of burning rubber and fat. They see Abraham, who tells them that he, too, was betrayed and forced at gunpoint to write the letter that sent Vladek and Anja to the camps. Vladek begins teaching English to his guard, who protects him and provides him with extra food and a new uniform. Mandelbaum is soon taken off to work and never heard from again. After a few months, the guard can no longer keep Vladek safe as a tutor, and he arranges for him to take a job as a tinsmith.

It is 1987, a year after the publication of the first book of Maus *and five years after Vladek's death. Art is depressed and overwhelmed, and visits his psychiatrist, Pavel, also a Holocaust survivor. The two speak about Art's relationship with his father and with the Holocaust. They focus particularly on issues of guilt. Art leaves the session feeling much better and returns home to listen to tapes of his father's Holocaust story.*

During this time, Anja is being held at Birkenau, a larger camp to the south. Unlike Auschwitz, which is a work camp, Birkenau is a waiting room for the gas chambers. Anja is despondent and frail, and her supervisor beats her constantly. Vladek makes contact with her through a kind Jewish supervisor named Mancie, through whom he is able to send additional food to his wife. Vladek also arranges to be sent to work in Birkenau, where he is able to speak briefly with Anja.

Vladek arranges to switch jobs from tinsmith to shoemaker, and by fixing the shoes of Anja's guard at Birkenau, he markedly improves her treatment. He learns that some prisoners at Birkenau will begin working at a munitions factory in Auschwitz and saves tremendous amounts of food and cigarettes for a bribe to ensure that Anja is among them. Soon, though, Vladek loses his job as a shoemaker, and he is forced into manual labor. He begins to get dangerously frail, and he must hide during daily "selections" so that he will not be sent to the gas chamber. As the Russians advance towards the camp, he works again as a tinsmith and is made to deconstruct the gas chambers.

The Russian army is now within earshot of Auschwitz, and the prisoners are evacuated under German guard. They march for miles in the freezing snow and are packed like rats into crowded boxcars, where they stay for days with no food or water. Eventually they arrive at Dachau, another concentration camp. Only one in ten prisoners survive this trip.

Vladek, Francoise, and Art drive to a grocery store, where Vladek attempts to return opened and partially−eaten food items. Art and Francoise wait in the car in embarrassment, but to their surprise, Vladek is successful.

At Dachau, Vladek meets a Frenchman who is able to receive packages through the Red Cross due to his non−Jew status. He shares this extra food, likely saving Vladek's life. Vladek eventually contracts typhus and lies close to death for days, until his fever begins to subside. Just as it does, the sick that are able to walk are boarded onto a train bound for Switzerland to be exchanged as prisoners of war. Vladek is among them.

On the way home from the grocery store, Francoise stops to pick up an African−American hitchhiker. Vladek is profoundly distrustful of blacks, and he is furious.

Vladek is made to leave the train and move on foot towards the Swiss border. The war ends before they reach it, and their guards march them back onto a train that they say will take them to the Americans. But when the train arrives at its destination, there are no Americans, and the prisoners walk off in all directions. Vladek is stopped by a German patrol and made to wait by a lake, where he meets his old friend Shivek. The Jews think that they will be killed, but when morning comes the guards are gone. Vladek and Shivek begin to walk again, but they encounter yet another German patrol, which forces them into a barn with fifty other Jews. Again, they fear for their lives, but when they awaken the next morning, the guards are gone. Vladek and Shivek eventually find an abandoned house, where they stay until the Americans arrive and take the house for military use.

Vladek shows his son a box of old photographs of his family, mostly from before the war. Of his parents and six siblings, only one brother, Pinek, survived.

Art is in his apartment when he receives an urgent and unexpected call from Mala. She is in Florida and back together with Vladek, though she does not seem happy about it. Vladek had just been admitted to the hospital for the third time in a month, and now he has left against the advice of his doctors. He wants to see his doctor in New York. Art flies down to help him get home. Back in New York, Vladek sees his doctor and is cleared to go home. A month goes by before Art visits his father again.

When he arrives, Mala tells him that Vladek has been getting confused. Art sits down on the end of his father's bed and asks him about the end of the war.

Vladek and Shivek leave the German farm for a displaced persons camp, where they receive identification papers. Life at the camp is easy, but Vladek soon leaves with Shivek for Hannover, where Shivek has a brother. While in Hannover, Vladek hears word that Anja is still alive, and he departs for Sosnowiec. The trains are largely incapacitated, and the journey takes him over three weeks, but he eventually arrives for a tearful reunion with his wife.

And here Vladek ends his story: "I'm tired of talking, Richieu," he tells Art, calling him by the name of his dead brother, "and it's enough stories for now."

Summary and Analysis of Book I, Chapter 1

Note: *Maus* jumps back and forth often between the past and the present. To facilitate these transitions in this summary, the Holocaust narrative is written in normal font, while all other narratives are written in italics.

The Sheik

The story begins with a brief prologue, set in Rego Park (Queens), NY, in 1958. The narrator, Art Spiegelman, at this point a small boy, is on roller skates, racing with his friends to the schoolyard. Art's skates break, and he runs crying to his father, Vladek. He tells his father that he fell and that his friends skated on without him. His father responds that until he has spent five days locked in a room with a group of people and no food, he cannot know the meaning of the word "friends."

It is 1978. Art greets his father at the old man's house in Rego Park. They are clearly not close, and they have not seen each other in some time. Vladek's first wife, Anja – Art's mother – committed suicide in 1968, and Vladek has since had two heart attacks. Vladek is a Holocaust survivor and has remarried a woman named Mala, who is also a survivor. The two fight constantly. Over dinner, Art tells his father that he wants to write a comic book about the old man's experiences during the Holocaust. Vladek mounts a stationary bicycle and begins to tell his story.

It is the early 1930s in Czestochowa, Poland. Vladek is young and handsome, and working in the textiles business. One day his friend introduces him to a girl named Lucia, and the two date for three or four years, but Vladek never feels particularly committed to the relationship. He travels to Sosnowiec, Poland, to visit his family in December of 1935, and is introduced to a girl named Anja, who is "clever, and from a good family." They hit it off, and though they live 40 miles apart, they begin to speak on the phone at least once a day. Anja send Vladek a photo of herself, which he places on his dresser. When Lucia sees the photo, the two end their relationship. Vladek and Anja are engaged at the end of 1936, and Vladek moves to Sosnowiec to live with his fiancé.

After the engagement, but before Vladek has moved to Sosnowiec, Lucia comes to his apartment and begs Vladek to take her back. Vladek refuses, and he does not hear from Lucia again. However, he also ceases to hear from Anja. When he calls, Anja's mother tells him that Anja received a letter from someone in Czestochowa that said horrible things about Vladek, including that he is only planning to marry Anja for her money. Vladek travels to Sosnowiec to address the situation. The letter is from Lucia, and after much convincing, Anja agrees to proceed with the marriage. They are wed in 1937, and they move into one of Anja's father's apartments. Vladek takes a share in his father–in–law's hosiery business.

Vladek tells his son that he does not want this part of the story in the book; it is too personal. Art promises not to include it.

Analysis

In Chapter 1, we learn that Art – both the author and the narrator of *Maus* – wishes to draw a book about his father's experiences during the Holocaust. Vladek begins his story shortly after, telling his son about his courtship and eventual marriage to his first wife, Anja. This chapter follows a structure that will soon become familiar, in which the story opens during a period between 1978 and 1982 (from here on referred to as the "present narrative") and then jumps to the past as Vladek continues his tale of Holocaust survival (the "past narrative"), before retuning again to the present. The past narrative is often briefly interrupted by small sections of present narrative. These past and present narratives represent the majority of the pages within *Maus*, and the pattern of "Present–Past–Present" is repeated in every chapter except for Chapter 2 of Book 2, which opens with a distinct third narrative (the "meta–narrative") before returning to the past.

Maus is really two stories, not one. The first story follows Vladek's experiences in World War II Poland, while the second story deals with Vladek's relationship with his son. Chapter 1 is an excellent introduction to this relationship: the two men are not particularly close, and they do not have an easy or relaxed manner around each other. One of the primary themes in *Maus* is that of *guilt*, which manifests itself a number of ways, such as in Art's feelings that he does not treat his father as well as he should. Evidence of this guilt appears on the very first panel of the first page. Art tells us that he hasn't seen his father in a long time, and that they are not particularly close. Upon his arrival, however, he gives his father an excited greeting – a disproportionate response resulting from the guilt he feels over his neglect of the old man.

Guilt is also present in another form within the pages of *Maus*. Throughout the book, we are subjected to the author's continuing obsession with the Holocaust: he feels that it has affected – and continues to affect – almost every aspect of his life. At various times in the story (notably in Book II, Chapters 1 and 2), Art tells us that this obsession existed even as a child. As described later in the story, much of this obsession stems from Art's feelings of guilt over having avoided the horrible events that both of his parents lived through. The opening prologue is the only part of *Maus* that shows Art during his childhood, and from this short scene, we can begin to see exactly why it is that the Holocaust plays such a dominant role in his psyche.

In the scene, ten–year–old Art breaks his roller skate and falls, and his friends skate on without him. This experience is fairly ordinary, and has played out in one form or another for thousands of ten–year–old boys and girls across the country. Most parents, when confronted with this situation, would offer words of comfort to their injured child. Vladek, however, immediately compares the situation to the Holocaust. Indeed, it seems likely that he compares almost *every* situation to the

Holocaust, cementing the events in the mind of his son. The scenes illustrates not only the reasons for Art's continuing obsession with the Holocaust, but also the fact that the events of the Holocaust are never far from Vladek's own thoughts.

Further evidence of the Holocaust's continuing impact on Vladek can be found if one compares Vladek personality in the late 1970s to his pre–Holocaust self. His relationship with Mala, his second wife, is clearly strained and loveless, and Vladek himself is somber and irritable. In the early 1930s, however, he is handsome and calm, and clearly filled with love for his first wife, Anja.

Summary and Analysis of Book I, Chapter 2

Note: *Maus* jumps back and forth often between the past and the present. To facilitate these transitions in this summary, the Holocaust narrative is written in normal font, while all other narratives are written in italics.

The Honeymoon

Art visits his aging father again in Rego Park. When he arrives, Vladek is dividing his pills into daily doses. In all, he takes over thirty pills a day, including six for his heart, one for diabetes, and more than twenty–five vitamins. He tells his son that prescription medications are only "junk food," and that to stay healthy, he must fight on his own. They sit at the table, and Vladek continues his story.

Before Vladek and Anja met, she had one other boyfriend, a Communist from Warsaw. A short while after their wedding, he returns to his apartment to find that the police have just arrested the seamstress next door. Anja had been decoding and relaying Communist messages from her old friend, and when she got word that the police would be coming, she took the messages over to her neighbor to hide. When the police arrived, they found the package and arrested the neighbor. The neighbor spends three months in jail, but is eventually released due to lack of evidence. After that incident, Vladek is ready to end his marriage, and he makes Anja promise that she will no longer consort with Communists.

Anja's father gives Vladek a factory to provide for his daughter and what he hopes will soon be their family. Their first child, Richieu, is born in 1937. He will not live through the war. Soon after giving birth Anja becomes terribly depressed, and Vladek takes her to an upscale sanitarium in Czechoslovakia. On the train, they look out the windows and see swastikas on flags in town centers and hear stories of rampant anti–Semitism. They are the first signs of the brewing Nazi storm. The sanitarium is beautiful, and Vladek takes good care of his ailing wife. They stay there for three months, and when they return she is much better.

When they return home, Vladek's father–in–law tells them that their factory was robbed while they were away. Everything was taken, though Vladek does not think that there were any anti–Semitic motives. Within a few months, though, they set up another factory, and soon things are again going well. They have a two–bedroom apartment and a Polish nurse. But anti–Semitic riots are brewing, and the situation is beginning to look ominous. The Nazis are stirring anti–Semitic sentiments amongst the Poles. Anja comments that, "when it comes to the Jews, the Poles don't need much stirring up." Their Polish nurse is offended and tells the Spiegelmans that she considers them family, but when things really begin to get bad, even the nurse will turn against them (see Book I, Chapter 6).

In 1939, Vladek receives a letter from the government drafting him into the army. He is sent west, to the German front.

Vladek drops his pills, blaming his eyes: one is made of glass, and the other has a cataract. He tells his son the story of when he was in the hospital for eye surgery. His surgeon left him to give lectures on television, and when his eye started bleeding, he was forced to run through the hospital looking for another doctor. Art seems uninterested.

Analysis

Art now visits his father "quite regularly," but it is clear that he is doing so mostly to hear his father's story. The first words out of Art's mouth when he sits down with his father are about Vladek's past, and for the most part it is all they talk about. At the end of the chapter, Vladek begins to talk about something else (his experiences with various eye diseases and doctors), and Art appears completely uninterested. Indeed, there are many times throughout *Maus* when Vladek begins to speak about a topic other than the Holocaust, but Art always quickly shifts the focus back to the past. This fact likely contributes to the guilt that Art continues to feel with regards to his neglect of his father.

This chapter provides further insight into Vladek's personality and the ways in which the Holocaust has shaped his life and his son's. Vladek takes a variety of pills and is clearly not healthy, suffering from both heart disease and diabetes.
Doctor–prescribed medication for these two ailments together totals seven pills, yet Vladek takes about thirty pills every day, the remaining pills comprised of various vitamins that he has read about in his "prevention magazines." As an explanation, he tells Art that "I must fight to save myself." This determination recalls his fight for survival during the Holocaust, another example of how the Holocaust, though forty years in the past, continues to have an effect on Vladek's personality and actions.

As the Holocaust is never completely out of Vladek's mind, it is not surprising that the Holocaust has also had a strong impact on his only son. In the prologue, we saw that Vladek mentioned the Holocaust to his son even when it was not particularly relevant (see Book I, Chapter I). In Chapter 2, we get the sense that even when the Holocaust is not mentioned explicitly, its influence is never far from Vladek's actions as a parent. While speaking with his son Vladek accidentally knocks over his bottle of pills, and his instinctual reaction is to blame Art. Later on, in Chapter 2 of Book II, Art's therapist suggests that Vladek feels guilty about surviving the Holocaust and takes this guilt out on his son. This incident with the pills is just one example; Art's childhood was likely filled with similar situations.

Chapter 2 also introduces the reader to the strict racial self–segregation that existed in pre–war Poland. In the sanitarium, we are confronted with images of striking racial diversity: Jews, Poles, French, Germans, and others share the same restaurant and dance floor. This diversity is the exception, rather than the norm. In this chapter

– and throughout the pages of *Maus* – all of Vladek's friends and acquaintances from pre–war Poland are Jewish. Non–Jewish Poles only appear within these pages as policemen or governesses, or in other lower–class, "blue collar" positions. It is clear that the Jews in Poland were on the whole wealthier than their non–Jewish countrymen. There are also many signs of a growing conflict between these classes. Communism, a theory that supports the idea of a classless state in which the common people control the means of production (factories, tools, materials, etc), has gained a foothold in the country, and Vladek returns from the sanitarium with Anja to find that his factory has been robbed. Anti–Semitism is also on the rise, indicating that the social, class–based unrest that is brewing is beginning to find a target in the Jews.

Summary and Analysis of Book I, Chapter 3

Note: *Maus* jumps back and forth often between the past and the present. To facilitate these transitions in this summary, the Holocaust narrative is written in normal font, while all other narratives are written in italics.

Prisoner of War

Art returns again to Rego Park to visit his father. Vladek is obsessed with Art finishing everything on his plate, just as he was when Art was a boy. Anja, though, would always eventually give him something he liked. Vladek tells his son that when he was twenty–one, his own father purposefully starved him and kept him deprived of sleep so that he would fail his army physical and not have to join along with the rest of the boys his age. The plan worked, but the army told him to work out for a year and then return. Vladek begged his father not to starve him again, and the next year he joined the army. Basic training was eighteen months, and he returned every four years for another month of training.

It is 1939, and Vladek has been sent to the German front. He sees a tree that seems to be moving and fires towards its center. It is a German soldier using branches for cover. The German falls and holds up a hand in surrender, but Vladek continues to shoot until he is dead. Vladek is soon captured and made to carry the German dead and wounded. He walks over to the river, finds the man he killed, and carries him back to be buried.

The Jewish prisoners are forced to live outside in tents in the bitter autumn cold and are fed only crusts of bread, while the Polish prisoners stay inside in heated cabins and receive two meals a day. Though it is cold, Vladek goes to the river every morning to bathe so as to keep away the lice that attacked so many of his comrades. To pass the time, he does gymnastics, plays chess, and prays. Vladek wakes up one morning to find a sign requesting workers and advertising good food and accommodation. He volunteers, and when he arrives at the camp, he is given his own bed and a full day to rest. The labor is hard work, literally moving mountains to flatten the terrain, and some men are too weak or old to do it.

One night, Vladek dreams of his grandfather, who tells him that he will be released from the camp on the day of Parshas Truma, a special event in the Jewish calendar. It is also a week of particular significance to Vladek: it was during this week that he was married to Anja, and it was also the week in which Art was born. Three months later it is Parshas Truma, and the prisoners are lined up in the main courtyard. He is made to sign a release form, and he is free to go. Vladek's dream about Parshas Truma has come true. He boards a train, which takes him through occupied Poland towards Sosnowiec, but the train travels past Sosnowiec (now officially part of Germany) and into the German–controlled government of the Reich Protectorate to the east (formerly central Poland). He is finally let off in Lublin, in the heart of the Reich Protectorate.

In Lublin, Vladek is led to a camp of large tents and hears stories about the last train of prisoners that arrived at the camp, from which six hundred Jews were marched into the forest and killed. Jewish authorities in the camp have bribed the guards to release prisoners into the homes of nearby Jews, and Vladek tells them that he has a cousin in Lublin. That night, Vladek leaves his tent to go to the bathroom and a guard begins to shoot at him. Vladek runs immediately back into his tent. The next morning the cousin arrives, and Vladek is set free. A few days later, he boards a train for Sosnowiec. He does not have the proper traveling papers, but by pretending to be Polish, he enlists the help of a Polish train conductor, who hides him from the German soldiers. He arrives first at his parents' house. His mother looks ill; she will die from cancer within a few months, thereby missing the worst of the Holocaust. His father, a very religious man, has been forced by the Nazis to shave off his beard. Vladek walks him over to Anja's apartment for a tearful reunion with his wife and son.

Art's father begins complaining about his relationship with Mala, claiming that everything would be better if Anja were still alive. Mala, he says, is always trying to take his money. Art looks for his coat, and Vladek tells him that he threw it in the garbage outside and that by now the garbage men have probably taken it. "Such an old, shabby coat," he tells his son. "It's a shame my son would wear such a coat."

Analysis

The scene at the dinner table provides yet another example of how the Holocaust has affected both Vladek and Art. Vladek's insistence that his son eat everything on his plate has its origins in his Holocaust experiences: he needed to eat whatever food he acquired in order to survive. This is particularly true in Auschwitz and the other concentration camps to which he is sent (Book II). These situations left him with an extraordinary aversion to wasted resources of any kind, and the preoccupation with food is only the first example of this (see, for example, the matches in Book II, Chapter I). As we have seen before, Art was directly affected by his father's thrifty impulses and his mother's more compassionate demeanor.

Interestingly, Vladek throws away his son's coat at the end of the chapter, behavior that stands in sharp contrast to his overwhelming compulsion to save. The best explanation for this seemingly uncharacteristic behavior lies in Vladek's reasons for saving. In discussions regarding his money and last testament (see, for example, Book I, Chapter 5), it becomes clear that Vladek wishes all of his money – hundreds of thousands of dollars saved over the forty years since the Holocaust – to be left to his son. His compulsive saving, then, reflects his desire for his son to live a good and prosperous life. Vladek is therefore offended by the sight of his son wearing an old and shabby coat, and he conspires to replace it with one that he thinks is better.

Chapter 3 also elaborates on the book's discussions of race and class. When Vladek boards a train from Lublin back to Sosnowiec, he is drawn wearing the mask of a pig, signifying that he is hiding his Jewish identity by pretending to be Polish. This concept of masks will appear again throughout the novel in similar fashion, as the Nazis begin to systematically exterminate the Jews, and Vladek and Anja are forced to go into hiding. The ease with which Vladek is able to assume the identity of a non–Jewish Pole is striking, considering the extremes of the Nazi racial stereotypes, and the incident highlights the irrationality of classifying people based on race. The role of masks is expanded later on in *Maus*, during the meta–narrative that begins Chapter 2 of Book II, in which all characters are portrayed as humans with animal masks. In this meta–narrative, the author suggests that race and nationality are only man–made classifications and that underneath these masks, we are all more alike than we are different.

Chapter 3 also includes Vladek's first – and only – mention of the Jewish religion within the pages of the story (with the exception of the "Prisoner on the Hell Planet" comic in Chapter 5 of Book I). Up until this point, the classification of Vladek, Art, and their friends and family as "Jews" is taken for granted and made concrete through their representation as mice, but the classification of "Jewish" seems to define a set of racial and cultural factors more than anything else. The Jewish *religion* is rarely mentioned. Freezing and starving within the confines of the prisoner of war camp, however, Vladek prayed every day.

Also in the camp, Vladek dreams of his grandfather, who tells him that he will be released on Parshas Truma, a week of the year corresponding to a specific section of the Torah. The day of Parshas Truma assumes a special significance to Vladek for the remainder of his life. However, he does not mention his religious faith again within the pages of *Maus*. The only other overt reference to religion occurs in Chapter 5 within the pages of the short "Prisoner on the Hell Planet" comic. Here, Vladek is shown praying in Hebrew over the casket of his dead wife. Vladek's religion manifests itself only in times of extreme stress and peril, and does not seem to play much of a role in his daily life. It is possible that Vladek's feelings towards the Jewish religion have been deeply affected by both the Holocaust and the death of his wife.

Significantly, while Vladek's father says he is religious, Art is not. He does not know the meaning of "Parshas Truma", for example. And later on, during the "Prisoner on the Hell Planet" comic, he recites from the Tibetan Book of the Dead during his mother's funeral, rather than from the Torah. This indicates a break in the transmission of religious faith from generation to generation.

Summary and Analysis of Book I, Chapter 4

Note: *Maus* jumps back and forth often between the past and the present. To facilitate these transitions in this summary, the Holocaust narrative is written in normal font, while all other narratives are written in italics.

The Noose Tightens

Art arrives again at his father's house in Queens, wearing a new coat. Vladek is upset: he had wanted his son to arrive earlier so that he could climb onto the roof and fix the drain pipe. Art has bought a new tape recorder for $75, and Vladek tells him that he could have found it elsewhere for much less. He continues his story.

It is 1940, and twelve people are living in Anja's father's house: Anja, Vladek, and Richieu; Anja's parents and one set of grandparents; Anja's sister, Tosha, her husband, Wolfe, and their daughter, Bibbi; and Lolek and Lonia, two children of Uncle Herman, who is in the United States. Food is strictly rationed by the Germans. Anja's parents had been donors to a Jewish charity organization, through which they are able to secure additional food. They buy the rest on the black market. All Jewish–owned businesses, including Vladek's factory, have been taken over by German overseers, and the family is living off of their savings. The Germans are looking for any excuse to arrest a Jew. Vladek meets an old customer of his, Mr. Ilzecki. He is still in business, making uniforms for soldiers. He tells Vladek to see him if he gets any cloth and hands him a note that will get him past the guards at his shop. Vladek visits shops that owed him money before the war and arranges to acquire some cloth, which he hides under his clothes and takes to Mr. Ilzecki in exchange for money.

Soon after, Vladek nearly escapes a German raid, in which they close off a street and take anyone without work papers. Anja's father bribes a friend of his who owns a tin shop to arrange for a priority work card for Vladek, so that he will be relatively safe during Nazi roundups. But things continue to get worse for the family. One day, Vladek is walking to see Mr. Ilzecki when he passes by a violent mob of German soldiers beating Jews to the ground with clubs and boarding them onto trains. He sees Mr. Ilzecki, who rushes him into his house, where they wait for hours for the trains to depart. The situation is so bad that Mr. Ilzecki is sending his son to hide with a Polish family until things get better. He suggests that Vladek do the same, but Anja refuses. Mr. Ilzecki's son will survive the war; Richieu will not.

In 1942, all Jews are forced to move into one quarter of town, and all twelve members of Vladek's family are assigned only two and a half small rooms. Vladek continues to conduct black market business until a friend of Anja's father is executed for selling goods without coupons and is left to hang for days as a warning to others. Vladek had often done business with the man, and he is terrified to go outside for a few days.

Art asks his father what Anja was doing during these times, and he responds that she was mostly doing housework, but that she recorded her whole story of the Holocaust in diaries after the war. Art tells his father that he wants to have those for his book.

Vladek begins dealing in gold and jewelry, which is easier to hide than clothing but still dangerous, and also does some business selling food. Business is still dangerous, though. On one occasion, Vladek is delivering a sack full of illegal sugar when he is stopped by a German patrol. Rather than run, he lies and tells them that he owns a grocery store and that he is carrying the sugar there, legally. He makes his delivery as planned, with the guards watching.

Soon, the family receives notice that all Jews over seventy years of age will be transferred to a new community specifically designed for the care of the elderly. Anja's grandparents are ninety. At the time, they have not yet heard of the concentration camps, but they do not want to be separated, so the family hides them behind a false wall in a storage shed. When police come looking for them, they are told that they left about a month ago without a word. But the police arrest Anja's father, and a few days later the family receives a note from him saying that if they don't give up the grandparents, the Germans will return to take more members of the family. The grandparents are taken away to Auschwitz.

A few months later, all Jews are ordered to report to the stadium for "registration," but people are suspicious of a Nazi plot. Vladek's father visits from a neighboring town. Vladek's mother has died of cancer, and he lives with his daughter, Fela, and her four small children. He asks his son for advice on what to do, but Vladek does not know. His cousin, Mordecai, will be at one of the registration tables, so perhaps he can help. Ultimately, almost everyone does show up at the stadium for fear of what would happen if they don't. There are perhaps 30,000 people at the stadium. Jews are told to line up and approach the tables to be registered. The elderly, families with many children, and people without work cards are sent to the left, while men of working age are being sent to the right. Vladek, Anja, and Richieu are spared. Vladek's father approaches Mordecai's table and is also sent to the right, but Fela and her four children are sent to the left. Realizing this, Vladek's father sneaks over to the left to be with his daughter, and none of them are heard from again. In all, maybe 10,000 people are sent to their deaths from the stadium.

Vladek has been on his stationary bike for some time, and he is feeling dizzy. He lies down to take a nap. Art walks into the kitchen, where Mala is smoking and playing solitaire. She tells him that her mother was also taken at the same stadium. Her mother was then taken to a complex of apartment houses that had been converted into makeshift prisons, to wait to be deported. The apartments had no food or toilets, and the cells were so crowded that people actually suffocated. Her mother survived this, and Mala's uncle, who was on the Jewish Committee, was able to hide her until all the trains had left. Both eventually died in Auschwitz.

Art walks into the living room with Mala to look for his mother's diary. His father never throws anything away, and the book shelves are crowded with old menus and useless junk. He cannot find the diaries. Art goes to leave, but Mala screams at him to put everything back the way he found it.

Analysis

The Nazi noose is beginning to tighten around the Jews of Poland. Anti–Semitic violence is increasing, and the Nazis are beginning to send the Jews to the concentration camps. In this chapter, Vladek's father and Anja's grandparents are all sent to Auschwitz. At the same time, Vladek is beginning to show the resourcefulness and thrift that will help to see him safely through the war. While the rest of Anja's family is living off of their savings, Vladek immediately begins to generate income by selling cloth on the black market. He gives half of his money to Anja's family, but always keeps half for himself. He is also extremely adept at thinking on his feet, a trait that saves him on more than one occasion.

Countless times throughout the story, Vladek's resourcefulness and quick mind help him to survive and to provide for is wife. However, these traits are ultimately not enough to save his life. However intelligent and resourceful Vladek is, his survival ultimately depends a great deal on *luck*. This is especially true as the situation deteriorates even further, but instances of luck can also be found in these early chapters. An excellent example of this is when he is caught carrying the black market sugar. Though he thinks quickly and devises a lie that fools the German soldiers, his survival in that situation was by no means assured; it was dependent upon the mood and intelligence of the soldiers and the reaction of the person to whom he delivered the sugar. Vladek's intelligence improved the odds in his favor, but his survival was nevertheless dependent on a roll of the dice.

In the present narrative, we continue to see that the Holocaust has changed Vladek, as the traits that helped him to survive still figure prominently in his personality, to the exasperation of his family. In Chapter 3, for example, he is preoccupied with Art finishing everything on his plate. Another example occurs in Chapter 4, when Art leaves his father to look for Anja's diaries in the library. The bookshelves are packed with useless items that Vladek cannot seem to throw away. This compulsion to save developed during the Holocaust: food and other necessities were scarce, and survival often depended upon one's ability to hoard. Forty years later, Vladek continues to save every item that might be of some use, however remote the possibility.

Yet there are also differences between Vladek's past and present selves. Chief among these differences is his overall demeanor. In the past narrative, Vladek is loving and kind in his relationship with Anja, and calm and composed in his dealings with other people. But there is no love in his second marriage to Mala, and the older Vladek is quick to anger and feels constantly imposed upon by those around him. At the end of this chapter, we hear some of Mala's survival story. Given that they both survived Auschwitz, it is interesting to compare their personalities. Mala endured similar hardships to those that Vladek faced, yet she does not share the personality traits that Vladek seems to have acquired during the Holocaust. The same can be said for Anja, whose experience was nearly identical to her husband's, yet, like Mala, Anja did not leave the Holocaust filled with bitterness and afflicted with a compulsion to save even the most frivolous items. How can two people who both experienced the same horrors have been affected so differently?

This question is raised by Art a few times over the course of the story, but a satisfactory answer is never provided. One possible explanation is the fact that while Vladek, Anja and Mala's Holocaust experiences may have been similar, the three found different ways to cope. For example, Vladek's survival was contingent on very different factors than Anja's. Though there was – as with all Holocaust survivors – a certain amount of luck involved in Vladek's survival, he relied to a large extent on his intelligence, resourcefulness, and ability to think on his feet. By comparison, Anja's survival depended predominantly on the kindness and resourcefulness of others. Before Auschwitz, she was almost completely dependent upon Vladek's ability to find food and shelter, and when she was separated from her husband in the concentration camps, she survived largely due to the kindness of her supervisor, Mancie.

Summary and Analysis of Book I, Chapter 5

Note: *Maus* jumps back and forth often between the past and the present. To facilitate these transitions in this summary, the Holocaust narrative is written in normal font, while all other narratives are written in italics.

Mouse Holes

It is 7:00 in the morning. Art is asleep in bed with his wife, Francoise, when the telephone rings. It is Mala, in hysterics. She tells Art that Vladek climbed onto the roof to try to fix the drain and then got dizzy and had to come down. Now, he wants to climb back up, and Mala is trying to talk him out of it. Vladek takes the phone and asks Art if he will come over to help. Art replies that he will call him back and hangs up. He tells Francoise that he has always hated helping his father out around the house. When he was a kid, nothing he did in that department was good enough for Vladek. One of the reasons he decided to become an artist was the fact that he wouldn't have to compete with his father. He would rather feel guilty than travel to Queens to help the old man fix the roof. When he calls his father back, Vladek tells him that his neighbor, Frank, has agreed to help him.

About a week later, Art visits his father again in Queens. Vladek is in the garage sorting nails, clearly upset. Art, feeling guilty, asks whether he can help, and his father curtly declines any assistance. In the kitchen, Mala tells Art that his father recently found a short comic that Art wrote years ago called "Prisoner on the Hell Planet," which told the story of his mother's suicide. In the comic, which is reprinted in full, Vladek arrives home to find Anja in the bathtub, her wrists cut and an empty bottle of pills nearby.

In the comic, the year is 1968. Art is 20, recently released from the state mental hospital and living with his parents. He arrives to find his father lying on the floor, a complete wreck. In accordance with Jewish custom, they sleep together on the floor, Vladek moaning through the night. Art is consumed by guilt. He thinks back to the last time he saw his mother, when she entered his room and asked him whether he still loved her. "Sure," he replied, and turned away. The comic ends with a message to his dead mother: "Congratulations, you've committed the perfect crime...You murdered me, Mommy, and left me here to take the rap."

Vladek walks into the room, and tells Art that the comic brought back painful memories of Anja, even though he is always thinking about her anyway. He isn't angry, only sad. Art and Vladek walk together to the bank, and Vladek continues the story of his Holocaust experience.

The year is 1943. All Jews are forced to leave Sosnowiec for a ghetto in the nearby town of Srodula. One night Persis, an uncle of Anja's brother–in–law, arrives. He is on the Jewish Council in a nearby town and wants to take Anja's sister Tosha, her husband Wolfe, and their daughter Bibbi to live with him in nearby Zawiercie, where he has some influence and thinks he can keep them safe. He wants to take Richieu with him as well, and Vladek and Anja agree. The parents watch as he takes Richieu away. It is the last time they will ever see him. A short time later, all the children in Srodula are rounded up to be killed, and the parents are glad that they have sent their son away, but the Zawiercie ghetto is liquidated shortly thereafter. Rather than be sent to the gas chambers, Tosha poisons herself, her children, and Richieu. Vladek and Anja are not made aware of this until much later.

In Srodula, the Germans begin to round up Jews at random. To protect himself and his family, Vladek builds a shelter under a coal bin, in which they hide during Nazi searches. Soon, though, they are moved to a different house. Again, Vladek builds a shelter, this time in the attic and accessible only through a chandelier in the ceiling. One evening, as they are leaving the shelter, they see a stranger below. It is a Jew, who tells them that he was only looking for food for his starving child. They think about killing him to be sure that he will not report them, but they take pity on him and give him some food. That afternoon, the Gestapo arrives and takes Vladek and his family into a secure compound in the middle of the ghetto.

The compound is a waiting area for transport to Auschwitz. Vladek enlists his cousin, Haskel, who is Chief of the Jewish Police, to help. In exchange for a diamond ring, Haskel arranges for the release of Vladek and Anja. Anja's parents also send valuables to Haskel, but in the end he chooses not to help them. At this point in the Holocaust, family loyalties have largely eroded, and it is every man for himself. They are transported to Auschwitz, where they eventually die. Haskel is a schemer and a crook, but he is well–connected and a good man to know in the ghetto. Every week, he plays poker with the German soldiers and intentionally loses so that they will like him. On one occasion, Vladek is out walking when he encounters a German guard who points a gun at his head and says that he is going to kill him, but when Vladek produces his papers and the guard sees that he is a friend of Haskel's, he is set free. Haskel arranges for Vladek to work in a shoe repair factory fixing the German soldiers' boots.

Vladek and Art are still walking to the bank when Vladek has an attack of angina, a pain in his chest caused by lack of blood flow to the heart muscle. He takes a Nitrostat pill and feels better almost immediately.

The Nazis continue to transport the Jews of Srodula to Auschwitz. Haskel arranges to smuggle himself out of the ghetto, but his brothers Miloch and Pesach have created a bunker behind a pile of shoes in the factory. Also around this time, Vladek and Anja finally hear the news of Richieu's death. Anja is hysterical with grief and tells Vladek that she wants to die. Vladek responds by telling her that "to die, it's easy…but you have to struggle for life." They retreat to the bunker along with about fifteen other people. There is no food. After many days, Pesach tells the group that he has bribed some guards to allow them to escape. Many in the bunker leave with him, but Vladek stays and watches as they leave the bunker and are shot by the guards. After a few more days, the ghetto is completely evacuated, and Vladek heads in the direction of Sosnowiec with his wife.

Vladek and Art arrive at the bank. Vladek wants to make a copy of the key to his safety deposit box for his son, so that if he dies Art can remove its contents before Mala can take it. In the box, Vladek has kept valuables from before the war, which he had hidden in a fireplace before being sent to the concentration camps. He retrieved them after the war, sneaking into the house in the middle of the night while the occupants slept. There is also a diamond ring in the box, which Vladek gave to Anja when they arrived in the U.S. Mala is obsessed with changing his will, he tells his son. Vladek wonders why he ever remarried and cries for the memory of his dead wife.

Analysis

The short interruption of "Prisoner on the Hell Planet" comprises an additional narrative voice in *Maus*, making a total of four voices (past, present, meta, and "prisoner"). The comic represents an entirely new and radically different artistic style than the simple and subdued style present throughout the rest of the book. The characters have distinctly human faces, and the drawings are marked by sharp angles, altered perspectives, and often surreal and grotesque human forms. But while the artistic style differs, it shares with *Maus* the theme of guilt. In "Prisoner on the Hell Planet" Art feels an unbearable sense of guilt over his mother's suicide, facilitated by the fact that his relatives seem to blame him as well. His cardinal sin, he feels, is one of neglect. This is poignantly driven home through Art's memories of the last time he saw his mother alive, when she came into his room and asked him if he still loved her. His answer, a dismissive "sure," is a constant reminder of his perceived neglect. Art's guilt over his mother's death is noteworthy for its similarity to the guilt that he feels regarding his father. This guilt is also based on neglect, and is highlighted at the beginning of this chapter, when Art refuses to help his father fix a leak on his roof.

In the analysis of the previous chapter, the question was posed as to why the Holocaust affected Vladek differently than Anja or Mala. One possible reason, explained in more detail in the previous chapter, is the fact that different people had different ways of coping with the horrors of the Holocaust. Vladek's means of survival – his resourcefulness and ability to use even the smallest of items for his benefit – clearly had an effect on his personality in later years. But while Vladek relied on his own resourcefulness, Anja relied primarily on others for her survival. Before she was taken to the concentration camps, she was almost completely reliant upon her husband for food and shelter. After the death of their son, it was Vladek who convinced her to live.

Anja's only post–Holocaust appearance within *Maus* occurs during the "Prisoner on the Hell Planet" comic, but though her appearance is brief, we can discern a great deal about her personality. In the comic, she is clearly depressed and on the verge of suicide. Her only line of dialogue is a question posed to her son, asking him if he still loves her. Art's response, a terse "sure," is far from reassuring. From this scene, we can surmise that Anja feels both alone and unloved. Cut off from the support of her family, she eventually kills herself. Just as she was dependent upon the kindness of others for survival during the Holocaust, her post–Holocaust personality is similarly defined by dependence. And just as Vladek's means of survival later manifested themselves in extreme forms, Anja's means of survival – her dependence on others – has manifested itself in a form so extreme that it eventually leads to suicide.

This chapter also deals with *survival*, another important theme of the book. As the Nazi brutality continues to worsen, the instinct for survival begins to overpower the powerful bonds of Jewish identity. This is first seen in the form of the Jewish Police. They are just as brutal as the Nazis, and almost indistinguishable from them save for the Stars of David on their shoulders. Vladek tells his son that some of these Jewish police felt that they could actually help the Jewish cause, but many joined in an attempt to save their own lives. The bonds of family break soon after, as Vladek's cousin, Haskel, will not help him without first receiving some form of payment. Says Vladek: "At that time it wasn't any more families. It was everybody to take care for himself!"

Summary and Analysis of Book I, Chapter 6

Note: *Maus* jumps back and forth often between the past and the present. To facilitate these transitions in this summary, the Holocaust narrative is written in normal font, while all other narratives are written in italics.

Mouse Trap

Art walks into his father's kitchen to see Mala crying at the table. She tells Art that his father treats her like a maid. Vladek gives her only $50 a month, and she is forced to use her savings for anything else she needs. He has hundreds of thousands of dollars in the bank but won't spend any money, even on himself. Art muses that he used to think that the Holocaust was what made Vladek so stingy with his money, but wonders why none of the other survivors have adopted similar personality traits. He confides to Mala that he is worried about how he is portraying his father in Maus, that in some ways, he has drawn him as a stereotypical, miserly, racist Jew.

Vladek walks into the kitchen, and Art shows him preliminary drawings from the comic he is writing about his father's Holocaust experiences. Both Mala and Vladek tell Art that the book will be special, but conversation eventually turns to bickering between Mala and Vladek over Mala's frequent trips to the hairdresser. Vladek tells Art that she is constantly threatening to leave, and his son suggests that they see a marriage counselor. Father and son go outside to sit in the garden and continue the story.

It is 1944, and Anja and Vladek are sneaking back towards Sosnowiec. Vladek can easily pass for a Polish man, but Anja has more traditionally Jewish features. They knock on the door of Richieu's former governess, who opens the door, recognizes the Spiegelmans, and then quickly slams it closed. Next they try Anja's father's old house. The janitor lets them in, and they are allowed to hide in a shed. Vladek goes out to find food and encounters another Jew in hiding, who leads him to a black market where they can buy supplies. Vladek returns with eggs, sausage, cheese, and other rare items.

Vladek returns to the black market again and encounters an old friend who tells him of a possible hiding place in the home of a Mrs. Kawka, at a farm just outside of town. They visit the farm, and Mrs. Kawka tells them they can stay in the barn, but they need to find another place in time for the coming winter. Vladek befriends a black market grocer, Mrs. Motonowa, who invites him to stay in her house with her and her son. Her husband is away for all but ten days out of every three months, and Vladek accepts.

Mrs. Motonowa charges for her hospitality, but she is a good woman, and her house is far better than the barn. One day, though, she is searched by the Gestapo and thinks that they may soon arrive at her house soon to search that as well. In a panic, she forces Vladek and Anja to leave. They wander the streets of Sosnowiec and eventually find a construction site where they spend the night. In the morning, they make their way back to Mrs. Kawka's and return to living in her barn. Mrs. Kawka tells Vladek of smugglers who will transport them to Hungary for the right price.

A few days later, back at the black market, Vladek runs into Mrs. Motonowa. She feels terrible about kicking them out and invites them back. Soon, though, her husband returns home for his vacation, and Anja and Vladek are forced to hide in the basement for ten days, with the rats and very little food. The husband eventually leaves and it is again safe to live upstairs, but Vladek does not feel entirely safe, and he resolves to search out the smugglers that Mrs. Kawka mentioned. On his way to the meeting, a group of small German children see him and run away screaming, calling out that he is a Jew. Rather than run, he has the presence of mind to approach the parents and patiently explain that he is a German and a loyal citizen of the Reich, likely saving his life.

When he arrives safely at Mrs. Kawka's farm, the smugglers are in the kitchen. Also in attendance are Mandelbaum, an old acquaintance of Vladek's, and Mandelbaum's nephew, Abraham. The smugglers explain their plan, and the Jews discuss it amongst themselves in Yiddish so that they will not be understood. They are not convinced of the smuggler's honesty, and in the end, Abraham decides to go and promises to write back if he makes it safely to Hungary. The rest will only travel if they receive the letter. Both Anja and Mrs. Motonawa are vehemently against the plan, but Vladek eventually overrules them both.

This issue thus settled, Vladek goes to visit Miloch, who is hiding in a garbage hole behind his old house with his wife and child. Vladek tells Miloch that he may soon be leaving for Hungary, and that there will be a vacancy at Mrs. Motonowa's. Soon after, Vladek, Anja, and Mandelbaum receive a letter from Abraham that says that he has arrived safely in Hungary.

Vladek, Anja, and Mandelbaum meet the smugglers at the train station, and they all board the train. After about an hour, however, they are arrested and stripped of their possessions. They have been betrayed by the smugglers. Vladek is made to board a truck with a hundred other prisoners and is transported to Auschwitz. Vladek and Anja are separated, not knowing if they will ever see each other again.

Art asks his father again about Anja's diaries, and Vladek says that they can't be found, because he burned them after Anja died. Vladek was depressed, and there were too many memories in those pages. All Vladek can remember about the content of the diaries is a sentence wishing that her son would one day be interested in them. Art is furious and screams at his father, calling him a murderer.

Analysis

As Art visits his father more and more, their relationship begins to change. In previous chapters, most of their communications focused around Vladek's retelling of his Holocaust experiences. Lately, though, their conversations have been getting more personal. At the beginning of Chapter 6, Vladek begins to complain again about his relationship with Mala, and Art suggests that they see a marriage counselor. This kind of honest assessment and advice has been uncharacteristic to date, and seems to be a sign that Art's frequent visits are leading to a more positive and open relationship.

However, as this chapter comes to a close, the relationship is strained almost to the point of breaking when Vladek tells his son that he burned Anja's diaries shortly after her death. And to add further insult to the tragedy, Vladek recalls that Anja once told him that she hoped Art would read them one day. At this, Art explodes at his father, calling him a "murderer." Though he apologizes, he leaves soon thereafter and again calls Vladek a "murderer" under his breath.

As seen in the "Prisoner on the Hell Planet" comic in the previous chapter, Art feels a terrible sense of guilt over his mother's suicide, and blames himself for not being a loving and attentive son. At the end of this chapter, however, Art seems to blame his father for his mother's death. There is a subtle difference between these two forms of blame. Art blames himself for his mother's physical death, but he blames his father for the murder of Anja's *memory*.

The history of the Holocaust is both the history of a genocide and the history of the individual deaths (and survivals) of millions of European Jews. The sheer magnitude of the horror – five million Jews were killed – is almost unimaginable, and yet each of those five million deaths represents an individual story. The Holocaust is therefore both a deeply personal and numbingly impersonal event. By destroying Anja's diaries, Vladek has made it impossible for his son to ever know the personal aspects of his mother's Holocaust experiences.

An additional point of note in this chapter is Art's decision to draw the different races as different animals. While Vladek and Anja are hiding in Mrs. Motonowa's basement a rat scurries across the floor, and Vladek tells his wife that it was only a mouse. The artist's depiction of the rat is anatomically correct, whereas his depiction of the Jews as mice is not: the Jews are drawn with the bodies of humans and the heads of mice. Similarly, Americans are portrayed as humans with the faces of dogs, while the Nazis use real dogs (with four legs, paws, etc.) to search for Jews in hiding. From this, it is clear that the author intends for the "races–as–animals" motif to be purely symbolic.

While the animal symbolism has been criticized as overly simplistic and for perpetuating racial stereotypes, the cat–and–mouse metaphor is an effective means of representing the Nazi–Jew relationship: the Nazis first "teased" the Jews, slowly taking away their freedom, before eventually killing them. Indeed, the idea of representing Jewish people as mice originated in Nazi propaganda, which portrayed Jews as a kind of vermin to be exterminated.

In addition to being an apt metaphor, the animal representations are a convenient means of visually representing the social and racial stratifications that existed during the war. And as an added benefit, the concept provides the opportunity to portray these relationships visually, without constantly resorting to words like "Jew," "German," and "Pole." However, as will be discussed below, the author himself expresses reservations about these animal metaphors in Chapter 2 of Book II.

Summary and Analysis of Book II, Chapter 1

Note: *Maus* jumps back and forth often between the past and the present. To facilitate these transitions in this summary, the Holocaust narrative is written in normal font, while all other narratives are written in italics.

Mauschwitz

Art is on vacation in Vermont, sitting under a tree and trying to decide how to draw his wife, Francoise, for her depiction in Maus. She is French, but she converted to Judaism before she married Art. He finally settles on a mouse. Just then, a friend runs up and says that Vladek has called to say that he has had a heart attack. They rush back to the house, and Art returns the call. But Vladek is not in the hospital: he only said that to ensure that Art would call him back. Mala, it seems, has left him, after taking money out of their joint account. He is almost hysterical. Art and Francoise head for the Catskills where Vladek is staying, packing light so that they have an excuse to leave.

In the car, Art tells Francoise about his complex feelings towards his father and the Holocaust. He has trouble relating to his parents' experiences, and sometimes he wishes he could have been in Auschwitz with them just so he could know what they went through. He feels guilty about having had an easier life. As a child he would sometimes think about which parent he would choose to have taken to Auschwitz; usually, he chose his father. He also tells Francoise about his complex feelings towards Richieu, the brother he never met. His parents used to keep a photo of Richieu on their bedroom wall. Existing only as a photograph and a memory, Richieu was the perfect child who could do no wrong, and Art felt himself in a strange rivalry with his "ghost brother."

They arrive at the Catskill bungalow late at night, and Vladek wakes up to greet them. He mentions that maybe they could stay the whole summer, but Art politely declines. Early in the morning, Vladek fills his son in on the details of Mala's departure. The final fight occurred at a bank, and involved issues of money, as usual. Now Mala is in Florida, where Vladek says she will try to get back the deposit on the condo they had been trying to buy. He is thinking of pressing charges. They begin to work on Vladek's papers. A few hours later, they are all very tense, and father and son seem on the verge of an argument. Francoise suggests that they go for a walk while she looks for the mistake in their calculations, and Vladek continues his story where he left off – at his arrival in Auschwitz.

At Auschwitz, the Nazis take his clothes, shave his head, and force him into a freezing cold shower. The prisoners thank God that it isn't gas. They are given clothes and shoes, many of which don't fit properly, and each prisoner receives a tattoo on the inside of his arm. There is a terrible, pervasive smell like burning rubber and fat, and there are smokestacks in the distance.

Vladek and Mandelbaum run into Abraham, who tells them that the smugglers had forced him to write the letter that brought Vladek and Anja to the camps at gunpoint. After this conversation, Vladek does not see Abraham again. However hard the Auschwitz experience is for Vladek, it is far more difficult for Mandelbaum. His pants are much too large, and his shoes are both the wrong size, one too large and the other too small. He needs to use one hand to hold up his pants and the other to hold a shoe in case he finds the chance to exchange it. He even loses his spoon when he drops it on the ground and someone else picks it up. Vladek and Mandelbaum sleep side–by–side on a single small bed.

The Polish supervisor – or Kapo – of their barracks lines up the prisoners and asks if anyone can speak English. Vladek is taken aside and left at a table full of food. After the meal, he begins to tutor the Kapo in English. He is then led into a supply closet full of clothes. He picks out some, and the guard also allows him to take a belt, spoon, and a pair of shoes for Mandelbaum. Mandelbaum is overjoyed, but soon the Germans take him to work, and Vladek never sees him again. For over two months the Kapo keeps Vladek safe, but soon he is told that he will need to be assigned to a work crew. He tells the Kapo that before the war he worked as a tinsmith.

Vladek and Art have walked to a private hotel, and Vladek says that they must sneak quietly towards the patio so that the guard does not see them. They settle at a table and join a game of bingo already in progress.

Analysis

Art's conversation with his wife in the car on their way to the Catskills is one of the most thematically important sections of the book. Art feels inadequate and poorly–equipped to finish the book he has set out to draw, and he is filled with complex emotions regarding his family and the Holocaust. This section introduces for the first time the concept of "survivor's guilt" and expands upon Art's relationship to the Holocaust.

In the car, Art discusses in some detail his preoccupation with the Holocaust. Art was born in Sweden after the end of the war, and was therefore spared its horrors, but it has deeply affected his life nonetheless. He thought often about the Holocaust even as a child, often imaging or wishing that he was in the camps with his parents. These details are part of a larger theme in *Maus* regarding *the impact of past events on the present*. This idea is prevalent throughout the story, as most of the main characters continue to be affected in one way or another by the Holocaust, which took place decades before Art began drawing Book I. Vladek, for example, is unable to throw anything away because his survival at Auschwitz depended on saving any objects that might prove useful.

For Art, this nexus of past and present is best represented by his relationship with Richieu. Vladek and Anja kept a photo of Richieu on their bedroom wall, and Art always felt that he couldn't live up to his "ghost brother's" image. But this prominent role of the past in Art's current life is reflected in other ways as well. Vladek, for example, continues to be affected by the specter of the Holocaust, which has in part given rise to personal qualities – stinginess, aversion to waste, etc. – that annoy and exasperate his son. The current relationship between Vladek and Art is perpetually strained in large part because of these qualities, and the tension weighs heavily on the son.

Guilt has to this point been a common theme in *Maus*, as Art attempts to deal with what he perceives to be his neglect or mistreatment of both Vladek and Anja. In the car with his wife, Art discusses a different kind of guilt. As he tells Francoise: "I somehow wish I had been in Auschwitz with my parents so I could really know what they lived through! I guess it's some kind of guilt about having had an easier life than they did." This guilt, stemming from having survived the Holocaust (or in Art's case never having to live through it) can be called *survivor's guilt*.

Survivor's guilt originates from two main sources in the book. The first, as mentioned above, is Art. The second, as will be discussed further in the analysis of the next chapter, is Vladek. In the following chapter, Art's therapist suggests that perhaps because Vladek himself felt so guilty about surviving, he subconsciously tried to make his own son share in the guilt. The guilt of these two men is therefore closely intertwined, and provides yet one more example of the immense impact of past events on the present lives of the main characters in *Maus*.

Another interesting point of note occurs at the very beginning of this chapter, as Art is sitting under a tree, trying to decide what kind of animal his wife should be in the book. She is French, but she is also Jewish, having converted before marriage in order to make Vladek happy. Art attempts to draw his wife as a frog (a common and somewhat derogatory term for the French), a mouse (because she's Jewish), a poodle (presumably a reference to a "French Poodle"), and many other animals. For her part, Francoise would prefer to be identified as a mouse. But when Art confronts her with her French nationality, she pauses and suggests a bunny rabbit. Art, however, rejects this portrayal as "too cute" to apply to a nation with a deep history of anti–Semitism and Nazi collaboration.

This exchange highlights a recurring difficulty in *Maus* of grouping diverse groups of people into rigid categories graphically represented by different animals. France may have an unsavory history, but should Francoise be held accountable for these events? There are good reasons for the author to represent ethnicities and nationalities as different animals. The cat/mouse motif is a good metaphor for German/Jewish relations, and the representations also allow for racial issues to be dealt with graphically, saving the need for messy identifications of race and nationality within the text. (In other words, when drawing a Jew, the author does not have to write in the text that the person is a Jew; he needs only to draw him or her as a mouse). But ethnicity and nationality are highly complex issues and at times the author's categorizations might seem overly simplistic. Indeed, the author himself has similar reservations that will be expanded upon in the next chapter.

Summary and Analysis of Book II, Chapter 2

Note: *Maus* jumps back and forth often between the past and the present. To facilitate these transitions in this summary, the Holocaust narrative is written in normal font, while all other narratives are written in italics.

Auschwitz: Time Flies

It is February of 1987, and Art is sitting over a drawing table smoking, now portrayed as a human in a mouse's mask. Flies buzz around his head. Vladek died of a heart attack in 1982, he writes, and he and Francoise are expecting their first child in a few months. The first book of Maus was published last year to great success, but he is feeling depressed. The image zooms out to reveal that Art's drawing table is sitting atop a pile of dead Jews from the concentration camps. He is overrun by interviews and profit–seekers. One asks him if there was any message in the book. Another proposes marketing an official Maus vest, patterned on the one that Art so often wears. As Art becomes increasingly overwhelmed, his image begins to transform into that of a small child.

He visits his psychiatrist, Pavel, also a Jewish survivor. He, too, is wearing a mouse mask. Art tells him that when he has time to draw, he feels mentally blocked from continuing the story. It seems to him that nothing he ever accomplishes will compare with his father's survival of the Holocaust. They begin to discuss Vladek's and Auschwitz's effects on Art. Perhaps Art feels remorse that he has portrayed his father in a less–than–positive light in his book, Pavel suggests; or maybe Vladek himself felt guilty about surviving Auschwitz when so many other people died and subconsciously passed this guilt to his son. They also discuss exactly what it means to have survived the Holocaust. If surviving is admirable, does that mean that not surviving is not admirable? Pavel tells Art that survival in the Holocaust wasn't based on skill or resources. Ultimately, it was random, based purely on luck.

As Art leaves his session, he grows from a small boy to an adult again. These sessions always seem to make him feel better. Art returns home and begins listening to the tapes he recorded of his conversations with his father. On one tape, Vladek is complaining to his son about Mala's constant attempts to get at his money, and Art, frustrated, yells at his father to continue his Holocaust story.

Vladek is working at the Auschwitz tin shop, though he has never been trained in this profession. Yidl, the chief of the tinmen, sees that Vladek doesn't know what he is doing. Yidl is a communist and despises Vladek's past as a factory owner, and Vladek becomes afraid that he will be reported. He arranges with some Polish workers – specialists from nearby towns – to trade for pieces of sausage, eggs, and bread, and he offers Yidl this food as a gift to smooth their relationship. Food throughout the camp is in short supply, and the rations of bitter tea, spoiled cheese, turnip soup, and bread – made from sawdust and flour – are insufficient. On top of the hunger, the guards are brutal. On one occasion, a prisoner yells to the guards that he is a German, not a Jew, and that his son is currently serving in the German army. In response, the guards take the man into an alley, push him down, and jump on his neck.

During this time, Anja is at Birkenau, a larger camp two miles to the south. Whereas Auschwitz is a camp for workers, Birkenau is just a waiting area for the gas chambers and crematoriums. Vladek maintains contact with his wife through a Hungarian Jewish girl named Mancie, who has a higher status at Birkenau because she is having an affair with an S.S. guard. Anja is frail and dejected, and contemplating suicide. Her Kapo treats her poorly, giving her jobs that she cannot perform and beating her when she fails. Mancie passes notes and food between the two, though to be caught in this offense would surely mean death.

When an S.S. guard comes to the tin shop looking for workers to go to Birkenau, Vladek volunteers on the chance that he might see his wife. The smokestacks at the camp are ever–present, lording over the buildings and constantly spewing smoke. When he arrives at the camp, he calls out for his wife and eventually finds her. She is very thin, and they speak without looking at each other so that the guards will not notice them. She tells her husband that she occasionally works in the kitchen and brings scraps of food out to her friends, and Vladek responds that she should save the scraps for herself. Everyone in the camps is looking out for their own survival, and not the survival of others.

At another meeting in Birkenau, a guard spots them speaking to each other and takes Vladek into an empty room, where he is beaten with a club and forced to count the blows. So far, though, Vladek is still relatively strong, and he is able to survive the daily selections where the weak are listed and later sent to the gas chamber. He vividly recalls one selection when one of his fellow prisoners had a rash and was taken off to one side to have his number recorded. The prisoner screamed all that night in the barracks, in fear of his impending death the next day. Vladek calmed him by telling him that everyone at the camp was going to die eventually, and that he must be brave. Besides, perhaps it wasn't even his turn yet. Sure enough, though, the guards arrived the next day to take the prisoner away.

In the tin shop, Vladek is still worried about Yidl, so when a need arises for a shoemaker, Vladek offers his services, having learned a bit about shoe repair while working in Miloch's shop. He makes excellent repairs, and officials prefer to send their shoes to him instead of to the larger shop in camp. Because of these repairs, he often receives gifts of food. Vladek learns that some of the prisoners at Birkenau will be sent to work in at a munitions factory in Auschwitz. In Birkenau, Anja is still having a terrible time, and her Kapo beats her at the slightest infraction. The Kapo's shoes, however, are falling apart, and Anja suggests she send them to Vladek in Auschwitz to be repaired. When the shoes come back, they are as good as new, and the Kapo treats Anja far better from that point on.

In order to arrange for Anja to be transferred to Auschwitz, Vladek saves food and cigarettes to bribe the guards. He keeps all that he saves in a box under his mattress, but one day it is stolen and he is forced to start over again. Eventually, though, he saves enough and Anja is brought over. Vladek throws packages of food to his wife, but one time she is spotted and chased into her barracks, where a friend hides her under a blanket as the guard searches from room to room. The guard is furious and makes the entire barracks run and jump and exercise until they are exhausted. It continues like this for days, but nobody turns her in. Vladek soon loses his job close to his wife when the tin shop is shut down. He is made to perform physical labor, carrying stones and digging holes, and he becomes dangerously skinny. On the next selection, he hides in a bathroom to avoid being sent to the gas chamber.

Father and son return from their walk in the Catskills, and Francoise meets them outside. She has finished the bank papers and made sandwiches for lunch. Vladek makes tea with a tea bag that he had used for breakfast and left to dry by the sink. He then continues his story.

When the Russians advance into Poland, the Nazis begin to disassemble the camp. Vladek is again made to work as a tinman, taking apart the machines in the gas chambers. Underground, there is a room for undressing, and the prisoners are made to believe they are going in for a shower. When they are undressed, they are herded into a shower room, also underground, and the room is filled with pesticides. The bodies are loaded onto an elevator with hooks and brought to ovens on the ground floor, where they are incinerated.

At this point, Art asks his father why the Jews didn't try to resist, and Vladek responds that everyone was tired, and that they couldn't really believe what was happening all around them. And there was always hope that they could survive until the Russians liberated the camp. If you tried to resist, you would surely be killed. Just then, Vladek drops a dish and it shatters. Art and Francoise clean up the mess, but Vladek tells them to save the pieces so that he can glue it back together. When Art offers to wash the remaining dishes, his father refuses, saying that his son would only break the rest of them.

Later that night, Francoise and Art are sitting on the porch after Vladek has fallen asleep. Art tells his wife that he hopes his father will get back together with Mala, if only because otherwise Vladek is his responsibility. Just then, Vladek begins to moan loudly in his sleep.

Analysis

The structure of Chapter 2 is unique, in that it does not follow the traditional Present–Past–Present trajectory. Rather, the chapter begins with a third type of narrative that can be referred to as a "meta–narrative." The chapter therefore follows a path of Meta–Past–Present. The meta–narrative takes place in 1987, one year after the publication of *Maus I* and five years after Vladek's death, and deals directly with

Art's doubts and worries about the book's publication. The section also goes into further detail regarding Art's still unresolved issues of guilt surrounding his father. The meta–narrative is one of the most thematically important sections of the book, with detailed examinations of many of the book's themes, especially *guilt, survival,* and *luck.*

One of the most striking features of this meta–narrative is a shift in the nature of the animal metaphor. In both the past and present narratives, all characters are drawn with human bodies and animal heads. In the meta–narrative, all characters are drawn as humans wearing animal masks, with the string clearly visible on the back and sides of their heads. Previous instances in the book have suggested that on some levels, the author considers the animal metaphor to be inappropriate and overly simplistic (see, for example, the discussion in the previous chapter about his decision to draw Francoise as a mouse). The meta–narrative, however, offers the most direct challenge to the validity of the metaphor on which much of the book is based. In other words, Art is having second thoughts about his decision to assign distinct animals to distinct races and nationalities. By placing all of his characters in masks, he is suggesting that issues of race and nationality are purely products of our minds, and that underneath we're all just people. Even though he is having second thoughts, he continues the metaphor throughout the rest of the story.

This section also includes one of the book's most powerful images: A depressed Art Spiegelman sitting at a drawing board balanced atop a pile of dead, emaciated Jews. Similar piles line the sidewalks outside of his apartment. These images are a haunting representation of the Holocaust's continuing effect on the author, and a reminder of the effects of the past upon the present. Despite the many years that have passed since the Holocaust, and despite the fact that he never lived through it himself, the events are a part of his everyday life.

Art's discussion with his psychiatrist delves further into these issues, focusing particularly on Art's guilt. Pavel suggests that Art feels guilty about his father's less–than–positive portrayal in *Maus I.* He then talks about survivor's guilt, suggesting that perhaps Vladek felt guilty about surviving the Holocaust when so many of his friends and family were killed, and that he took this guilt out on his son. This idea of Vladek's own guilt is never corroborated by Vladek personally, but there are instances in the book in which we can see this transference take place. Perhaps the best example of this occurs during the brief prologue to Book I, which takes place in Queens, when Art is ten years old. In the scene, Art is roller skating with his friends when his skate breaks and his friends go ahead without him. When he comes crying to his father, Vladek only admonishes him and says that until he has been locked in a room with a group of people and no food for a week, he cannot even know the meaning of the word "friend."

Art's therapy session also delves into a discussion of survival and luck. Pavel asks Art whether it is admirable to have survived that Holocaust, and by the same token, whether it is *not* admirable to have *not* survived the Holocaust. In the end, says

Pavel, all survival was random and based purely on luck. Though Vladek clearly possesses many qualities that helped him to survive the Holocaust – resourcefulness, the ability to save food and money, etc. – his survival was nevertheless dependent upon a great deal of luck. Instances of this luck are everywhere, and many examples can be found within this chapter. When Vladek becomes too skinny to pass the daily selections, for example, he hides in the bathroom, and is never discovered based purely on chance. Similarly, when the guard sees him speaking with his wife, he is severely beaten. Prisoners in Auschwitz were killed for far lesser offenses, and the fact that his life was spared was again based purely on chance.

Summary and Analysis of Book II, Chapter 3

Note: *Maus* jumps back and forth often between the past and the present. To facilitate these transitions in this summary, the Holocaust narrative is written in normal font, while all other narratives are written in italics.

And Here My Troubles Began

The next morning, Vladek begins packing up the food that Mala left so he can return it to the store. Since the Holocaust, he says, he can't seem to throw anything away. He tries several times to give his son some of his extra food, but each time Art refuses, quickly rising into anger. Vladek asks his son to stay with him in the Catskills until the end of the summer, but Art and Francoise both agree that they will only be there for a few more days. They drive to the store, sitting three–across in the front seat of the car. Art asks his father about something he read about Auschwitz, about prisoners working in the crematorium who revolted, killing three guards and destroying the building. Vladek responds that while the story is true, the conspirators were later killed, and the young girls that supplied the ammunition were hung just outside of his workshop.

The Russian army is now very close, and the sound of artillery can be heard in the distance. The Nazis plan to take all prisoners into the heart of Germany, but a friend of Vladek's contrives a plan to escape. When the Germans move to take everyone away, they will hide in an unused attic until the camp is evacuated. To prepare, Vladek arranges to acquire civilian clothes for himself and his co–conspirators, and each day they save half of their food to store in the room. During the final days of Auschwitz, they hide in the attic to avoid detection. During the evacuation, however, rumors fly that the Nazis will set fire to the entire camp and bomb the buildings after they leave. Vladek and his friends fear for their lives and leave the camp with the rest of the prisoners and guards. The camp is never bombed.

They are marched for miles through the woods in the freezing snow. Those who cannot walk fast enough are shot. Some of Vladek's friends from the attic bribe the guards to allow them to escape, and they ask Vladek to join them. Vladek refuses, and when the time comes for the escape, his friends are shot in the back as they run. And so he is marched into Germany to Gross–Rosen, a small camp with no gas chambers. The next morning, they are forced onto a train and packed shoulder–to–shoulder, perhaps two hundred to every car. Vladek still has a thin blanket with him and is able to attach it to some high hooks to create a makeshift hammock. He sits above the shoulders of his fellow Jews for the duration of the ride.

The train travels for some time, and then stops for many days. There is no food or water. Vladek is able to reach through a window and survives on snow from the top of the car. One man in the car with Vladek has some sugar, but when he eats it, it burns his throat. He pleads to Vladek for some snow from the roof, but Vladek will only give him some in exchange for some sugar. Only about twenty–five people make it out of the train alive. The doors are eventually opened, and the prisoners are made to throw out the dead and clean the cars. There are many other trains whose doors were never opened, and are filled with the dead. Soon, they are herded back into the train. Each day, the Nazis open the doors to remove more bodies, and the car becomes more spacious. The train again begins to move, and again they are left for days with no food or water. Then, improbably, the doors open and they are greeted by the Red Cross. Each man receives a cup of coffee and a piece of bread before being herded back onto the train, which they now know is headed for Dachau.

They arrive at the grocery store. Vladek wants to return some opened and partially–eaten food, and Art and Francoise wait in the car, embarrassed and unwilling to participate. They see Vladek and the manager shouting at each other through the store window. Eventually, though, he returns to the car victorious, having received six dollars of groceries for only one dollar. He tells his son that the store manager was happy to help once he told him about the Holocaust, Mala's departure, and his current poor health.

Dachau is extremely crowded, and the prisoners lie huddled in the locked barracks. The straw in the barracks is full of lice, and the lice carry typhus. In order to receive food, all prisoners are forced to remove their shirts for inspection before every meal. If the shirt has lice, they are denied food. Unfortunately, it is almost impossible to escape the lice. Vladek's hand becomes infected, and he cuts at it to make it worse so he can move to the infirmary, where there is food three times a day and everyone has their own bed. He continues to irritate his infection daily, but he is eventually discovered and allows his hand to heal. He still has the scar.

Back at the barracks, Vladek is approached by a Frenchman who is looking for somebody he can talk to. Nobody in the camp speaks any French, but the man does speak a little English. The two talk each day to pass the time. Because he is not a Jew, he is allowed to receive packages, and he shares the food he receives with Vladek, likely saving his life. By trading some of the Frenchman's food, he is able to secure for himself an extra shirt, which he washes thoroughly and keeps in a piece of paper. During meal times, he changes into the clean shirt so that he can pass the lice inspection.

After a few weeks, however, Vladek contracts typhus, a deadly disease from which many others will die in Dachau. He must travel back and forth to the restroom, walking through a crowded corridor and stepping on the bodies of the dead. Eventually he is carried to the infirmary, where he lies for days, too weak to eat and close to death. Still, he saves his food and uses it for bribes. His fever eventually goes down, and shortly afterward a guard arrives informing the sick that anyone well enough to travel should line up outside to be exchanged as prisoners of war. Vladek is still weak, but he bribes other prisoners with bread to help him down from his bed and across to the train, which takes him towards Switzerland.

In the car on the way back from the store, Vladek tells his son that he exchanged letters with the Frenchman for years, but burned them along with Anja's diaries. Francoise stops the car to pick up a hitchhiker, an African–American. Vladek is furious and mumbles to himself in Polish. When the hitchhiker is let out, Vladek screams at Francoise about letting a "schvartser" into the car who might have stolen their groceries. His prejudice originates from his first few days in New York after the war; he says that blacks would steal his belongings if he left them unattended.

Analysis

After Vladek was separated from Anja for the last time before their reunion at the end of the war, all his instincts focused on one thing: survival. It was now truly every man for himself, as he was marched through freezing woods and packed into a boxcar with two hundred other prisoners. Vladek was able to eat the snow from the roof of the car, but he did not give any to the other prisoners unless they had something to trade in return. Likewise, later on when Vladek was sick with typhus and needed to walk to a train so that he could be released as a prisoner of war, he had to bribe someone to help him; they would not help for free. The frantic struggle to survive had largely broken the common bonds of humanity, religion, and friendship that previously held the Jewish community together.

What is even more striking about this breakdown is the fact that during the final days of Auschwitz and subsequent tribulations in the train cars and at Dachau, Vladek did not once mention Anja. He never once appeared to worry about her survival, nor did he attempt to include her in his escape plans from Auschwitz. Part of the reason for this is likely the fact that including his wife in his own plans was simply not possible. Anja was in Birkenau, while Vladek was in Auschwitz, and the bribes that would have been required to bring Anja to Auschwitz would have been too much even for Vladek to save. But it would also appear (at least from Art's re–telling of Vladek's story) that during his most difficult times, even his thoughts for his wife were supplanted by the struggle for his own survival.

Against this backdrop of self–preservation in which even the most fundamental human bonds were severed, the few occasions in which prisoners displayed pure altruism became particularly memorable. Perhaps the only example of altruism in the face of the Holocaust's most difficult times is found in Mancie, Anja's companion at Birkenau. Though passing notes and food between Vladek and his wife could very well have gotten her killed, she did so without accepting any payment. And, as Vladek tells his son in the next chapter, Mancie continued to keep Anja by her side through their own long and cold march from Birkenau, likely saving her life.

It is also interesting to note that the author's drawings of Jews are virtually indistinguishable from one another, especially when they are all wearing the same prisoner's uniform or when they are naked. In drawing the mice this way, Art Spiegelman is calling attention to the fact that the Holocaust can be thought of in two different ways: both as a faceless genocide, and as the individual murders of five million people. In *Maus*, we are reading an isolated account of one man's Holocaust survival, and yet this story was not an isolated event. The Holocaust did not just happen to Vladek, but to an entire race of people. Similar stories unfolded for millions across Europe, and Vladek's account is only one among many. In other words, Vladek's story is not unique, in much the same way that the facial characteristics of Spiegelman's Jews are not unique.

Also of note in this chapter is the fact that Vladek, the victim of perhaps the most horrendous application of mass racism in the history of civilization, is himself a racist, as evidenced by his reaction to picking up a black hitchhiker. His feelings towards African–Americans are the result of his experiences during his first few days in New York City; he felt that they were always trying to steal his valuables. From this, Vladek has judged an entire race of people in much the same way that the Jews were condemned during the Holocaust (albeit on a much smaller and less violent scale).

Summary and Analysis of Book II, Chapter 4

Note: *Maus* jumps back and forth often between the past and the present. To facilitate these transitions in this summary, the Holocaust narrative is written in normal font, while all other narratives are written in italics.

Saved

It is autumn in Rego Park. Clearly lonely and depressed, Vladek talks to his son about money, wondering why he has saved his whole life if all he has now is diabetes and an emergency oxygen bottle. He asks Art again to move in with him, and Art once again refuses, telling his father that he should find himself a live–in nurse. Ending this conversation, Vladek asks his son for help putting in the storm windows in his house, but Art delays, asking his father to tell him more about the Holocaust. He asks his father how Anja survived the end of the war. Though Vladek's memories of this are not so clear, he tells his son that she was taken from Auschwitz earlier than Vladek and marched through Gross–Rosen, all the while being kept safe by Mancie. All Vladek really knows is that she was eventually released close to Russia and then made her way back to Sosnowiec. After the war, he looked hard for Mancie to express his gratitude, but he never found her.

Vladek is taken on a train towards the Swiss border to be exchanged for prisoners of war, and is given a Red Cross package filled with food. It is a passenger train with seats, in contrast to the cattle cars of the last train in which he traveled. However, before the train reaches border they are made to get out and walk towards the frontier. On their way, they are stopped by their guards and made to stand in place for hours. Then the news arrives: the war is over. But they are not released. Instead, they are marched towards another train which they are told will take them to the next town, and to the Americans. The train is unguarded, but when it stops a half hour later, the Americans are nowhere to be found. Rather than wait, the former prisoners walk off in different directions. Soon, Vladek is stopped by a German army patrol and forced to walk towards a lake, where he encounters his old friend, Shivek, and several other Jews. They don't know what is going to happen to them. There are machine guns set up all around them, and they fearfully wait through the night, certain that they will be killed. But when they wake up the next morning, the Germans are all gone, having even left their machine guns.

Vladek and Shivek walk away, but they encounter yet another German patrol that forces them and perhaps fifty other Jews into a barn, where they wait through another anxious night. There is machine gun fire all around them, but the next morning they awake to find that once again, their guards have left in the middle of the night. Vladek and Shivek walk out to find somewhere safe to hide and encounter a gruff German civilian who tells them that they can hide in a hole behind his house. They lie there for a day, until a Nazi officer drives by and asks the civilian for directions. He provides them, but then also informs the officer that Vladek and Shivek are hiding out back. The officers, in too much of a hurry to bother, continue on their course, but Vladek wisely decides that it is best to leave.

They come upon an empty house and climb up into a hay loft in the barn. From the loft, they see that many of the town's citizens are running away, and they suddenly hear a loud explosion as the Nazis blow up a bridge to aid their escape. In the house, they find milk, chickens, and clothes. They stay there for days, dressed as civilians and killing a chicken each day for food. Eventually the Americans arrive, and they are safe. The house will be part of the American's base camp, but Vladek and Shivek are allowed to stay if they keep the place clean and make the soldiers' beds. The Americans are friendly: they call Vladek "Willie" and give him and Shivek gifts of food. One day the former owner of the house returns and accuses them of stealing her husband's clothes. Vladek and Shivek are made to return the clothes that they are wearing, but they do not worry, since they have filled three suitcases with more.

Back at Rego Park, Vladek shows his son a box of old photographs that he obtained from Richieu's governess after the war. They sit on the couch and Vladek tells his son about the people in the photos. On Vladek's side of the family, out of his mother, father, and six siblings, only his brother, Pinek, survived. Lolek, Vladek's nephew who was with him the Srodula ghetto, survived Auschwitz and later became an engineer and college professor.

Just then, Vladek has a pain in his chest. He takes a nitrostat pill, and the pain goes away. He is tired, though, and lies down on the couch to rest, leaving the storm windows for another time.

Analysis

Throughout *Maus*, Art has been feeling guilty at what he perceives to be his neglect of his father. Chapter 4 opens and closes with scenes that would appear to support this perception. Vladek's health is clearly deteriorating, and when Art first arrives, Vladek, concerned about how he will get by with Mala gone, asks his son to move in with him for awhile. Art almost shouts his negative response to his father, a scene that has been repeated in other chapters (e.g. Book II, Chapter 3). Living in such close quarters with his father is clearly not an option for Art, and he would prefer that his father spend the money to hire a nurse to look after him. Though he has his reasons, if faced with a choice Art would rather inconvenience his father than inconvenience himself.

The same can be said regarding the storm window insulation, for which Vladek requires the help of his son. Rather than help his father, Art instead asks Vladek to tell him more about his and his wife's experiences during the Holocaust. After speaking for some time, Vladek experiences severe chest pains and must stop his story and rest. The storm windows must wait for another day, but Art refuses to return until the following week, preferring for his father to "pay a bit more for heat for a few days longer" than for himself to be inconvenienced. Similarly, though Vladek often wishes to discuss his relationship with Mala and his deteriorating health – issues critical to him in the present – his son often forces the conversation back to the past – issues that are more critical to the completion of Art's book. Sensing this, Art lamely apologizes to his father at the end of the chapter for asking him to "talk so much." He does not, however, apologize for his other displays of selfish behavior.

When Art first asks his father to continue his Holocaust story in this chapter, he urges Vladek to "tell me more about Anja," referring to his mother's experiences in surviving Auschwitz. Vladek, however, interprets the question differently: "What is there to tell?" he asks. "Everywhere I look I'm seeing Anja." Here we can see that the Holocaust is not the only event in Vladek's life that has deeply affected him. The death of his wife also continues to affect Vladek on a daily basis. This has been seen in other sections of the book as well; for example, during Vladek and Art's walk to the bank Vladek breaks down in tears over the memory of his wife. Though it would be unfair to say that Vladek's personality has been entirely shaped by these two events, they have been by far the dominant forces in his life. The extent to which each of these forces has shaped Vladek's personality is an interesting and complex question that is not satisfactorily answered in the text. Indeed, these two forces are in many ways related, and a clear answer to the question may not even be possible. Nevertheless, it is useful to discuss this issue in a little more detail.

Anja had a long history of depression. After Richieu was born, she sunk into a deep depression and was forced to leave home for three months to recover in a sanitarium. She also expressed despair after her nephew, Lolek, decided that he was tired of hiding and allowed himself to be taken to Auschwitz. Her despair focused on the fact that much of her family had been taken from her in one way or another by the Holocaust. She repeatedly told Vladek that she no longer wanted to live. A third instance of Anja's depression occurred at Birkenau, where she told her husband that she often thought about killing herself by running into the electric fence. Viewed in this light, Anja's eventual suicide should have come as no surprise.

In all of the above cases, however, Vladek was there for Anja to give her strength and see her through these difficult times, each time drawing her away from her self–destructive thoughts. After the Holocaust, however, Vladek changed: he no longer displayed the loving warmth that characterized his pre–Holocaust relationship with Anja. Perhaps a variable that distinguishes Anja's previous suicidal thoughts from her actual suicide was the support of her husband. With much of her family dead, she was left with only Vladek and Art for support. As seen in the "Prisoner on the Hell Planet" comic in Chapter 5 of Book I, Art was not much support at all. Perhaps this colder Vladek was equally unsupportive of his wife. If this was the case, then it is likely that Anja's suicide left Vladek with a considerable amount of guilt, in addition to the guilt that he already feels for having survived the Holocaust while so many other people died.

Chapter 4 closes with a powerful scene in which Vladek shows his son photos of his and Anja's family. Most of their relatives died in the Holocaust. Out of Vladek's six siblings, only his brother Pinek survived, and Vladek visibly sags under the weight of so much death. The Holocaust destroyed nearly his entire family, and all that he has left are these photos. Pinek survived by deserting the Polish army and taking shelter with a family of peasant Jews. He had been traveling with their brother, Leon, but Leon eventually died of typhus. That Leon died from the same disease that Vladek contracted at Dachau once again underscores the critical role that luck played in determining who survived and who died during the Holocaust. Both brothers caught typhus; only one survived.

Summary and Analysis of Book II, Chapter 5

Note: *Maus* jumps back and forth often between the past and the present. To facilitate these transitions in this summary, the Holocaust narrative is written in normal font, while all other narratives are written in italics.

The Second Honeymoon

Vladek is in Florida, and Art worries aloud to his wife about how he will take care of his father. Moving to Rego Park is still out of the question, and there is no way that Vladek could move in with him and Francoise since they live in a fourth floor walk–up apartment, and Vladek's heart would not be able to handle it. The phone rings, and it is Mala. She is back together with Vladek, and she is calling to tell Art that his father has been admitted to the hospital with water in his lungs for the third time in a month. Art hangs up and calls the hospital, but Vladek is not there. Worried, he calls Mala back, and she tells him that Vladek left the hospital against the advice of his doctors. He looks sick and says that he does not trust the doctors in Florida; he wants to see his own doctor in New York.

Art flies to Florida to help Mala with his father. When he arrives, Vladek is lying in bed, breathing with the help of an oxygen unit. Art has arranged for emergency oxygen on their flight back to New York, and for an ambulance to pick them up at the airport. Art asks Mala how and why the two got back together, but she says that she doesn't know. She seems as unhappy as ever, and now Vladek is even more difficult than he was a few months ago. The next morning, everything is packed. Art and Vladek sit outside on deck chairs, and Vladek tells his son about the period of time just after the war, during which he moved to Sweden with his wife to await a visa to the United States. He took on labor jobs for a while but eventually used his resourcefulness and natural sales abilities to work his way up to become a partner at a Jewish–owned department store. Their visas arrived a few years later, and the family moved to New York, where he made a living selling diamonds.

Vladek, Art, and Mala prepare to board a flight to New York later that day. The plane is delayed six hours before takeoff, and when it finally comes time to board, Vladek complains that his oxygen unit isn't working, and that he cannot breathe. The crew tells them that Vladek is too sick to fly, but they refuse to leave the plane. Eventually Vladek checks his oxygen unit again and says that it is working, and the plane takes off. An ambulance meets them at the airport (a half–hour late), and Vladek is taken to the hospital. His doctor performs thorough tests and decides that he can go home. Art was hoping that his father could stay in the hospital, but he takes his father back to Rego Park, where Mala is waiting.

About a month later, Art visits his father again for the first time since Florida. Vladek often gets confused these days, and they are preparing to sell the house and move to Florida permanently. Art sits down by his father's bed to record the final chapter of his story.

Vladek is staying with Shivek on a farm that the Americans are using as a base. Eventually, they are made to relocate to a camp for displaced persons, At the camp, Vladek gets a fever, and the doctors tell him that he is having a relapse of typhus. The fever subsides, but Vladek is told that something else is still not right. A year later, he is diagnosed with diabetes. Vladek and Shivek eventually leave for Hannover, where Shivek has a brother. There are no passenger trains, but they board a freight train towards the city. The tracks are often broken, and the trip is long as the trains are forced to make constant detours through war–torn Germany. When they finally arrive in Hannover, Shivek's sister–in–law suggests that Vladek go to a large camp nearby to look for word of his wife. At the camp, he sees two girls from Sosnowiec, who tell him that Anja is alive, but that Sosnowiec is still a dangerous place, as there are stories of Poles continuing to kill Jews after the war has ended.

Undeterred, Vladek sends her a letter and makes his way back to Sosnowiec. With the letter he also sends a photo of himself in concentration camp–style pinstripes, which the photographer had ready for "souvenir photos." The trip through Poland takes three or four weeks. He eventually makes his way to the Sosnowiec Jewish Organization, and he is reunited with his wife, "such a moment that everybody around was crying together."

With this, Vladek ends his story. "I'm tired of talking, Richieu," he tells Art, calling him by the name of his dead brother, "and it's enough stories for now."

Analysis

For the most part, the author's drawings of Jews have been almost completely generic, consisting of nothing more than eyes, mouth, nose, and whiskers. By making all Jewish people look alike, Spiegelman has thus far created the impression that the Holocaust happened to a mass of anonymous people. By drawing the Jews as mice rather than as people, he has removed the reader's ability to fully identify with the main characters of the story. Though *Maus* is a story about people (as opposed to mice), the nature of the drawings adds distance between the reader and the characters. The photo of Vladek Spiegelman on page 134 changes all of this in an instant. What could once have been read as the story of an anonymous mouse becomes the story of a man with a face. By showing us this photo, the author forces the reader to reconsider the terrible events of the previous pages in a different light, as all the pain and suffering become associated with the man in the photo. Though the story to this point has certainly been poignant and emotional, the photo allows the reader to more closely empathize with the Vladek and his experiences.

The photo also forces readers to reconsider the way they think about the millions of people whose lives have been affected by the Holocaust. The amount of death, destruction, and pain is almost unimaginable, and contemplation of the total number generally creates a sense of a faceless mass of victims, much like the mice in *Maus*, who all look essentially the same. By showing the face of one of the Holocaust's victims, readers are asked to think about the Holocaust in terms of its effects on millions of individuals, each with their own friends, families, loves, and ambitions. Seen in this way, the tragedy of the Holocaust is multiplied exponentially.

The photo of Richieu in the acknowledgements of Book II has a similar – though slightly different – effect. Vladek, for his part, survived the Holocaust, but he did not emerge completely unscathed: he lost most of his family, and his personality was been forever altered by the terrible events. Richieu, on the other hand, did not survive the Holocaust. His photo, in contrast to Vladek's, is a reminder that those who *died* should likewise be thought of as individuals.

Vladek's last words underscore serve as a final reminder that the events of the Holocaust have had a lasting effect on the people who lived through it. By accidentally calling Art by the name of his son who died in the Holocaust, he betrays the fact that the events are never far from his mind.

Suggested Essay Questions

1. Though the author was born in Sweden after the end of the Holocaust, the events have nevertheless had a profound effect on his life. Discuss the nature of these effects and why the Holocaust remains such a formative event.
2. What is the significance of the author's decision to portray people of different races and nationalities as different animals? What effect does this have on the understanding and impact of the story?
3. *Maus* is written in the rather unconventional form of a graphic novel. Is this format an effective means of telling a Holocaust narrative? How might it differ from a more conventional Holocaust narrative?
4. To what degree was Vladek's survival based on luck, and to what degree was his survival based on his considerable resourcefulness?
5. To what extent are Vladek's aggravating personality traits a product of his experiences during the Holocaust?
6. Discuss Art's portrayal of his father. Is it a fair portrayal? What feelings does Art have about this portrayal?
7. Throughout *Maus*, Art is consumed with guilt. Discuss these different forms of guilt. How do they relate to one another? How do they differ?
8. The second chapter of Book II of *Maus* begins with a third level of narrative, which takes place in 1987, nine years after Art began working on *Maus* and five years after the death of his father. What is the purpose of this narrative, and what does it tell us about the author's relationship with his father and with the Holocaust?
9. Compare Vladek's marriage to Mala with his previous marriage to Anja. Why is Vladek's relationship with Mala so contentious, while his relationship with Anja was so filled with love?
10. Though *Maus* focuses largely on the Jewish people, the narrative generally avoids issues of religion. To what extent are the major characters religious? What role does religion play in their lives?

Questions of Genre in Maus

Combining the unlikely elements of comic books and the Holocaust, Art Spiegelman's *Maus* is a truly unique work of art. As a medium, comics are generally associated with superheroes and wacky characters; at first glance, using a comic book format for a topic as terrible as the Holocaust might appear to be in poor taste. Yet *Maus* ultimately succeeds in portraying the horrors of that event and speaking to the shadows that it continues to cast on survivors and their children.

Just as *Maus* defies conventions in its combination of medium and subject, it also defies definition in terms of genre. When it was first published, the *New York Times* placed the book on the fiction bestseller list, but Spiegelman requested that it be moved to the non–fiction list. On other occasions, however, the author has called *Maus* a work of fiction. Indeed, the book encompasses many genres simultaneously, and remains decidedly unclassifiable. The paragraphs below explain how *Maus* relates to the genres to which it has variously been ascribed.

Biography: *Maus* consists of two primary narratives. One of these follows Vladek's experiences in the Holocaust, while the other follows Vladek's relationship with his son, Art, who is also the author of the book. Vladek's story is told directly to his son in a series of interviews, which are then translated into the comic book form by the author. In this sense, Vladek's Holocaust narrative is largely a biographical work, tracing his experiences and those of his family from pre–war Poland to Auschwitz to his eventual return home. Indeed, in 1986, *Maus* was nominated for a National Book Critics Circle Award under the category of "Biography."

Autobiography: In the same way that Vladek's Holocaust narrative can be considered a biography, the second primary narrative of the story, in which Art details his relationship with his father, can be called an autobiography. There are actually two levels of autobiography within the pages of *Maus*. The first takes place between 1978 and 1982 and illustrates the series of interviews during which Vladek told his son about his Holocaust experiences. The second level of autobiography takes place in 1987, one year after the publication of the first volume of *Maus* and five years after Vladek's death. This section details the author's feelings regarding the book's publication and his ongoing attempts to make peace with both his father and the Holocaust. Both autobiographical sections are deeply personal, relating not just events but also the complex feelings and emotions that form the basis of many of the book's themes.

History: Before and during Spiegelman's work on *Maus*, the author conducted extensive research into the Holocaust so that the graphic representations of his father's story could be as accurate as possible. Due to this combination of research and personal narrative, *Maus* provides a startlingly realistic impression of Holocaust life not just for Vladek, but also for millions of other Polish Jews, thereby elevating the story from "biography" to a form of "history."

Fiction: While *Maus* incorporates many aspects of non–fiction, the book also contains many elements commonly reserved for fictional works, including the frequent use of metaphor, symbolism, and allegory. In addition to these elements, Vladek's story is passed through many filters, revisions, and interpretations before it is conveyed to the reader. The nature of the story's transmission (from Vladek's experiences, to his memory, to his son, to the drawing board, to the reader) generates the very real possibility of inaccuracy and subjectivity. In Spiegelman's own words:

> I'm all too aware that ultimately what I'm creating is a realistic fiction. The experiences my father actually went through [are not exactly the same as] what he's able to remember and what he's able to articulate of these experiences. Then there's what I'm able to understand of what he articulated, and what I'm able to put down on paper. And then of course there's what the reader can make of that. (*Oral History Journal*, Spring 1987)

Author of ClassicNote and Sources

Jack Murphy, author of ClassicNote. Completed on January 17, 2007, copyright held by GradeSaver.

Updated and revised Jordan Berkow January 28, 2007. Copyright held by GradeSaver.

Deborah R. Geis (ed.). Considering Maus: Approaches to Art Spiegelman's "Survivor's tale" of the Holocaust. Tuscaloosa, AL: University of Alabama Press, 2003.

Marie–Laure Ryan (ed.). Narrative across media: The languages of storytelling. Lincoln, NE: University of Nebraska Press, 2004.

Dominick LaCapra. History and Memory After Auschwitz. Ithaca, NY: Cornell University Press, 1998.

Joseph Witek. Comic books as History: The Narrative Art of Jack Jackson, Art Spiegelman, and Harvey Pekar. Jackson, MI: University of Mississippi Press, 1989.

Ian Johnson, Malaspina University. "On Spiegelman's Maus I and II." 2001–12–28. 2007–01–17. <http://www.mala.bc.ca/~Johnstoi/introser/maus.htm>.

Essay: Stylistic Detail of MAUS and Its Effect on Reader Attachment

by Sarah Yao
February 07, 2004

In any artistic work, aesthetic style is a crucial aid to the viewer's understanding of the piece as a whole. Art Spiegelman's remarkable publication Maus breaks the conventional barriers of the past between comics and what were then considered to be serious novels. As a graphic novel about a horrific atrocity, Maus is the first work of its kind. Through the style of his drawings, Spiegelman is able to use illustration to aid in the telling of a story. Each individually crafted panel is detailed enough to be significant alone; together, they create a rich tapestry of images which portray a powerful story without compromising the work's literary integrity. Page 87 of Maus is an ideal example of Spiegelman's combination of thoughtful detail and underlying meaning in his drawings.

In panels 2, 3, 6 and 7 of page 87, Vladek and Artie are only shown as silhouettes. This might be taken to represent a connection with Vladek's past. As Adolf Hitler is quoted to have said, "The Jews are undoubtedly a race, but they are not human," Jews were not viewed as worthwhile individuals. As the camps and gas chambers filled, each Jew became only a number, if even that. As the Jews were faceless then, Vladek is depicted as being faceless in the present.

Yet, it is noteworthy that Vladek's glasses are still visible against his dark silhouette. Glasses stereotypically represent a person's thought and intellect, and in these panels, spectacles imply a hint of Vladek's human aptitude. The contrast between the glasses and the silhouette is an ironic detail beyond what the initial glance might discern. Thoughtful details like these that appear throughout Maus are significant in their ability to lend a sense of humanity to an inhumanly cruel tale. Almost six million Jews were massacred during the Holocaust; although many works have been written about and around the events of the Second World War, Spiegelman, through the use of image, attempts through new venues to help the reader relate. In Maus, the people – often victims of history – are revived, transformed and metamorphosed into hand–drawn characters. Although these comics, because they are inherently two–dimensional, cannot do complete justice to multi–dimensional human beings, they do not deviate far from the truth.

Perhaps for entertainment value, or to an extent, to alleviate the grim nature of his novel, Spiegelman adds a caricature–like quality to the depiction of his characters, particularly Vladek, who becomes the stereotypical Miserly Jew. This almost laughable quality is most obvious in the novel when Vladek, who – even in his advanced age – continues to carry home small knickknacks and bits he finds along the street, refuses to part with a piece of wire he discovers while strolling with his son. Vladek is additionally depicted as being petty and unforgiving, harsh in speech and uncouth in manner, and somewhat a bigot. However, it is ironically also these personality flaws that cause his rodent–faced character to appear more real, more "human." As the reader comes to silently despise Vladek for his numerous shortcomings, he becomes increasingly attached to the character on an unconscious level. This unconscious concern for the character later translates into compassion and sympathy, and gradually the thoughtful development of Maus's characters causes us to almost forget that even Vladek has a rodent tail. In the telling of the story, as Jews are mice, not inherently harmful but reputed pests requiring riddance, Nazis are given cat faces, somewhat menacing, but strangely more physically resembling humans than those of their rodent counterparts.

As the reader becomes drawn deeper into the tale and closer to the characters, drama within the plot takes on increased effect. By page 87, the reader has already witnessed the setting of the scene for the entrance of concentration camps into the story. On page 86, the suspense and shock build; the individual panels are larger in size than those of previous pages, particularly than the noticeably smaller frames of page 85. It is worthy to note that in most of the book's pages, especially those preceding pages 86 and 87, the mice are not depicted to have visible eyebrows. However, on 86, the expressions of anxiety and fear created by the shape of the mice's suddenly present eyebrows dominate the page. This evokes an air of anticipation in the reader, which carries over into the next page. Here, on page 87, as if finally reaching a crescendo, the panels in which Vladek recalls the past to Artie show the two figures as silhouettes only. Drama becomes heightened; it is comparable to the effect created when the face of a camp side storyteller is illuminated with the single beam of a flashlight. These silhouette panels could even be called negatives, similar to photo negatives, as the color of the subjects and backgrounds are reversed. In film, this type of inverse of light and dark lends a feeling of apprehension, foreshadowing doom of some kind. Despite the intense drama of the page, it is appropriate – this is the first time in Maus that Vladek and his family are directly affected by the events at Auschwitz.

Although the story of the Holocaust has been told countless times, and in the present day, the occurrences at concentration camps have all been exposed, it is with such subtle details that Spiegelman is able to persuade the reader into shock when Maus characters begin to be exterminated. The reader is forced to rely increasingly on the posture and gesticulations of the figures, Valdek's in particular, and on the dialogue. Especially on page 87, many words are printed in bold lettering. This deviates from previous pages, which have few or no bolded words. Again, these small, easily dismissible coincidences can be proven to be in actuality not coincidences at all, but carefully planned components of the graphic novel.

Maus is a refreshing transgression from the norm. As art, it is impressive in its magnitude; as literature, it propels story telling to new venues. Art Spiegelman has proven that not only can two media of expression be combined successfully; they can be united without detriment to either artistic or literary integrity. He is most commendable, however, not for that which readers notice, but for that which they easily overlook – the subtle yet powerful details that permeate his work, leaving readers breathless without them realizing exactly why.

Essay: Stylistic Detail of MAUS and Its Effect on Reader Attachment

Essay: Using Animals to Divide: Illustrated Allegory in Maus and Terrible Things

by Anonymous
December 09, 2004

Today, most Americans can only imagine what the horrors of the Holocaust must have been like – and, to be frank, they are probably very glad that they have no personal experiences to draw on. However, the Holocaust, and other catastrophic events in history, must be remembered. Even as Americans who live nowhere near the places that were ravaged by destruction and genocide, we must attempt to understand the Holocaust, because even events as horrific as the genocide of Jews in Europe are a part of history – and history tends to repeat itself. Many authors of Holocaust literature seem to believe that awareness equals prevention. Both words and images are a vital component of remembrance, as exemplified by allegorical Holocaust literature such as that created by authors Art Spiegelman and Eve Bunting. Art Spiegelman, in his *Maus* books, and Eve Bunting, author of the children's book *Terrible Things: An Allegory of the Holocaust*, show us that words and images are both essential in representations of the Holocaust. The use of an allegory in which animals symbolize people, when paired with careful style and pattern choices for illustrations, is highly effective in conveying the message that racism and division can lead, quite simply, to "terrible things".

Maus is an unusual account of the Holocaust – it is strikingly different from most Holocaust literature targeted at adults, yet Spiegelman's work has attracted an amazing number of readers of all ages. In fact, *Maus* won the Pulitzer Prize in 1992, and has proven to be a staple in many college classrooms. In writing and illustrating *Maus*, Art Spielgelman took on the difficult task of accurately representing his father's story, as well as depicting the things that Vladek told him in a way that the public could understand and appreciate. Interestingly, he chose to represent people in *Maus* as animals, with each race portrayed as a different animal. In this allegory, the Jews are depicted as mice, the Germans are cats, the Poles are pigs, and when Americans are introduced in *Maus II*, they are dogs. Besides creating an obvious division between some of the key groups in the Holocaust, readers can read more deeply into Spiegelman's choice of animal for each race. The cat and mouse idea behind the portrayal of the Germans and the Jews is a fairly obvious one. Speigelman's choice to draw the Poles as pigs, however, could be taken in several ways: perhaps they are depicted as pigs because they stand by and do nothing while the Jews are taken away, or perhaps the pig symbolizes the Poles' greed and selfishness when they took over Jewish homes and businesses after the Jews were evacuated from Polish towns. Either way, Speigelman's depiction of these four races pushes readers to recognize the racial differences, hatred, and segregation that occurred during the Holocaust, and his allegory proves to be a poignant one.

Throughout *Maus* and *Maus II*, Speigelman uses metaphors to spotlight the division between races in Europe at the time of the Holocaust. His two volumes follow Vladek's story from a time when he was a normal citizen of Poland, to a time when Jews, Poles, and Germans each had their distinctive places in society, and finally to a time when Jews were slaughtered simply for the fact that they were Jewish. Speigelman's depiction of Jews as mice helps readers who may know little about such extreme racism to understand that the differences in appearance, dialect, and the like were the primary signs that the Nazis used to direct their hatred. In the Holocaust all of the European races were human; similarly, in Maus all of the characters are animals, yet it is the subtle differences between them that cause the death of millions.

When Vladek must take his wife Anja to the sanitarium, Speigelman illustrates a perfect world in which all animals can live in harmony. Though it is ironic that everyone is only at peace when they are in a sanitarium, this is the only time in his two volumes that Speigelman brings all the different kinds of animals together. Here, there are mice, pigs, cats, and dogs, as well as rabbits, horses, giraffes, goats, and frogs. Once they leave the sanitarium and enter the "real" world again, however, racism rears its head and they separate once again. It is interesting that Speigelman chooses to send the message that only in a completely contrived, unnatural situation such as a "health resort" can different races be truly at peace, but nonetheless, this adds to the strength of his allegory.

Bunting's *Terrible Things* also uses animals to symbolize groups that were persecuted during the Holocaust. She and illustrator Stephen Gammell create a forest filled with rabbits, squirrels, fish, birds, frogs, and porcupines. All of the animals live together peacefully until the Terrible Things come to the forest and wreak havoc on nature's harmony. The Terrible Things are not represented as animals, as the Nazis are in *Maus*, but rather as ethereal, haunting shadows that blot out the sun. The first time the Terrible Things come to visit, they say, "We have come for every creature with feathers on its back." All of the animals of the forest say, "We don't have feathers" – except, of course, for the birds, who are then taken away. Upon each return, the Terrible Things take away another type of animal, while the ones who do not meet the criteria look the other way, glad that they are able to stay in the clearing. The Terrible Things continue to come back, however, until they have taken away all the animals except for the white rabbits. Little Rabbit is afraid and wants to move, but Big Rabbit counters, "Why should we move? This has always been our home. And the Terrible Things won't come back. We are the White Rabbits. It couldn't happen to us." Then, of course, it does: the white rabbits are taken away, all except for Little Rabbit who is small enough to hide in the rocks. In the end, Little Rabbit realizes that, "If only we creatures had stuck together, it could have been different."

Speigelman's metaphor for racism is echoed in *Terrible Things*, and here it is especially effective in teaching young children that no matter how different people are, bad things can happen to anyone. The book's message is that it is important to stick together and try to help each other rather than ignore each others' suffering.

Terrible Things differs from *Maus*, however, in that each race is not associated with a specific animal. Also, the Nazis, or the Terrible Things, are not represented as animals, but rather as ominous clouds lurking over the forest. *Terrible Things* is more abstract than *Maus*, in that the animals do not represent particular groups (most likely because such references would most likely be lost on children, the intended audience); here, the allegory here focuses on obvious differences that children can see (feathers, color, ability to swim, etc.). Each group of forest animals has distinct differences, and each time the Terrible Things come to take some of them away, the animals that remain are very glad that it is not their turn. Though this story may be disturbing to younger children, it is effective at alerting readers that differences between people should not cause such division that they allow terrible things to happen. As Bunting states as a sort of preface to *Terrible Things*, "In Europe, during World War II, many people looked the other way while terrible things happened. They pretended not to know that their neighbors were being taken away and locked in concentration camps. They pretended not to hear their cries for help. The Nazis killed millions of Jews and others in the Holocaust. If everyone had stood together at the first sign of evil, would this have happened?" Bunting invites children and adults alike to think about the consequences of their own actions and prejudices, and Gammell's illustrations throughout *Terrible Things* inspire the same discomfort and sadness in children that Speigelman's images of hatred and death in *Maus* inspire in adults. So, image paired with word, we see here, can make a big impact.

Images can communicate things that even words cannot, and are especially relevant in the context of Holocaust literature. In representing the Holocaust through images, it is important to consider factors such as style, color, and placement. As an illustrator one must consider the effect that the illustrations will have on the viewer, and both Spiegelman and Gammell made choices that enhance comprehension in the reader and convey a clear message. Both illustrators portray their subjects in simple black and white, and both make the pictures take over each page in such a way that they become the main focus of the books. The use of black and white is convincing for depictions of the Holocaust, even when animals are the subject, because any real photographs that readers may have seen from the era would have been black and white. Black and white is often used to convey the gravity of a situation, as well, and using these shades to illustrate *Maus* and *Terrible Things* allows Speigelman and Gammell to create serious, somber messages about the possible consequences of hatred. Also, images take center stage in these books presumably because the story behind Holocaust is really about the people, about the victims, and about what happened to them, rather than merely an account of the number of dead bodies or a history of how Hitler came to acquire such power.

With all their similarities, however, there are some marked differences between the two illustrators' styles. While Spiegelman uses thick black lines and a comic book format, Gammell uses pencil drawings and a more realistic style. Both illustrators' images are full of impact, though, because the pictures command such a power and presence on the page. The lack of color draws the reader to the image and begs them to analyze what they are seeing. For example, Gammell includes an image of a frightened squirrel who is about to be captured by the Terrible Things. Children reading this book will immediately notice the squirrel's expression of fear because Gammell places the detailed creature so carefully on the page. In *Maus II*, likewise, Speigelman captures the expressions of burning bodies in the gas chambers of Auschwitz, and his use of bold lines captivates, horrifies, and consumes the reader. Also, in each book, the animal allegory adds to the impact of the pictures because for very young children who may not be able to handle images of real bodies, depictions of animals can serve as a gateway to understanding the true story of the Holocaust. Seeing these illustrations may be quite upsetting to children, and when they learn later that these things happened to humans, they will be able to assimilate the feelings they had when reading *Terrible Things* into what they are learning about real victims. Also, the allegory works to impact adult readers of Maus when they see Speigelman's drawings because the characters do clearly represent actual humans.

In the end, *Maus* and *Terrible Things* leave readers feeling something powerful. Whether it is sadness, shock, or a determination to never again ignore the pain of others, Speigelman and Bunting have both created very poignant works. Using both words and images, these authors have done something that many Holocaust writers have not – they have connected the words that many have heard about the Holocaust with images that make sense to their intended audience.

Quiz 1

1. **How does the elder Vladek exercise?**
   A. Lifts weights
   B. Roller blading
   C. Goes for a run
   D. Stationary bicycle

2. **In what city did Vladek live before he met Anja?**
   A. Bielsko
   B. Srodula
   C. Sosnowiec
   D. Czestochowa

3. **Who introduces Vladek to Anja?**
   A. His father
   B. His mother
   C. His cousin
   D. His brother

4. **What is Vladek's business before he meets Anja?**
   A. Manufacturing
   B. Tinsmith
   C. Textiles
   D. Shoe Repair

5. **How does Lucia get revenge on Vladek when she hears of his engagement?**
   A. She writes an incriminating letter to Anja
   B. She gets him fired from his job
   C. She steals money
   D. She trashes his apartment

6. **To whom does Anja give Communist documents for hiding?**
   A. Her father
   B. Lucia
   C. Her neighbor
   D. Vladek

7. **What does Anja's father give to Vladek to assist with his career?**
    A. A munitions factory
    B. A shoe factory
    C. A textile store
    D. A textile factory

8. **In what country is the sanitarium to which Anja is brought after she becomes depressed?**
    A. Poland
    B. Russia
    C. Germany
    D. Czechoslovakia

9. **When Vladek and Anja return from the sanitarium, what has happened to their factory?**
    A. It has been taken over by the Germans
    B. It has been robbed
    C. It has been sold to a competitor
    D. It has burned to the ground

10. **At what age did Vladek first go into the army?**
    A. 16
    B. 18
    C. 21
    D. 25

11. **What did Vladek's father do to try and prevent his joining the army?**
    A. Pulled out his teeth
    B. Intentionally starved him
    C. Bribed an army officer
    D. Moved to a different country

12. **How many Germans does Vladek kill in the one battle he fights?**
    A. 1
    B. 2
    C. 5
    D. 10

13. **What does Vladek eventually do to the soldier he kills?**
     A. Writes to his family
     B. Takes his watch
     C. Buries him
     D. Says a prayer over his body

14. **What stands out about Vladek's hands when they are examined by a German soldier?**
     A. They are very delicate
     B. They are scarred
     C. They are thoroughly scratched
     D. They are calloused

15. **What does Vladek do every morning at the P.O.W. camp?**
     A. Takes a bath in a nearby river
     B. Writes a letter to his family
     C. Smokes a cigarette
     D. Says a prayer

16. **What game do the P.O.W.s play at the camp?**
     A. Cribbage
     B. Checkers
     C. Backgammon
     D. Chess

17. **At the P.O.W. camp, who visits Vladek in a dream?**
     A. His grandfather
     B. His father
     C. His mother
     D. Anja

18. **In Vladek's dream at the P.O.W. camp, on what day will he be released?**
     A. Rosh Hashanah
     B. Parshas Truma
     C. Passover
     D. Yom Kippur

19. **To what city is Vladek brought when he is first released from the German P.O.W. camp?**
    A. Lublin
    B. Bielsko
    C. Breslin
    D. Sosnowiec

20. **What happened to the previous group of prisoners released from the P.O.W. camp?**
    A. They were placed in another P.O.W. camp
    B. They were shot
    C. They were forced into a ghetto
    D. They were sent to a concentration camp

21. **Who claims Vladek as a cousin to guarantee his release at Lublin?**
    A. Mandelbaum
    B. Lolek
    C. Wolfe
    D. Orbach

22. **What does Vladek see has happened to his father when he returns from the P.O.W. camp?**
    A. He has suffered a heart attack
    B. He has suffered a stroke
    C. He has been sent to a concentration camp
    D. The Germans have cut off his beard

23. **What does Vladek do to Art's coat?**
    A. He takes it for himself
    B. He throws it away
    C. He spills food on it
    D. He asks Mala to fix it

24. **What chore does Vladek ask Art to help him with on his third visit to Rego Park?**
    A. Rake the leaves
    B. Clean the garage
    C. Fix a drain pipe on the roof
    D. Do the dishes

25. **When Vladek returns to Sosnowiec from the P.O.W. camp, how many people are living in Anja's father's house?**

A. 2

B. 5

C. 12

D. 15

Quiz 1 Answer Key

1. **(D)** Stationary bicycle
2. **(D)** Czestochowa
3. **(C)** His cousin
4. **(C)** Textiles
5. **(A)** She writes an incriminating letter to Anja
6. **(C)** Her neighbor
7. **(D)** A textile factory
8. **(D)** Czechoslovakia
9. **(B)** It has been robbed
10. **(C)** 21
11. **(B)** Intentionally starved him
12. **(A)** 1
13. **(C)** Buries him
14. **(A)** They are very delicate
15. **(A)** Takes a bath in a nearby river
16. **(D)** Chess
17. **(A)** His grandfather
18. **(B)** Parshas Truma
19. **(A)** Lublin
20. **(B)** They were shot
21. **(D)** Orbach
22. **(D)** The Germans have cut off his beard
23. **(B)** He throws it away
24. **(C)** Fix a drain pipe on the roof
25. **(C)** 12

Quiz 2

1. **On his first trip to the black market upon his release from the P.O.W. camp, who does Vladek encounter?**
   A. Mr. Ilzecki
   B. Mandelbaum
   C. Mr. Lukowski
   D. Mrs. Motonowa

2. **How does Vladek begin earning money after he is released from the P.O.W. camp?**
   A. He sells off his father-in-law's possessions
   B. He sells textiles on the black market
   C. He sells food on the black market
   D. He starts working at the factory he used to own

3. **To prevent being taken away by patrolling Germans in Sosnowiec, where does Vladek acquire work papers?**
   A. A grocery store
   B. A tinsmith
   C. A textile factory
   D. A shoe repair store

4. **Who is the first person to offer to take Richieu to safety?**
   A. Mr. Ilzecki
   B. Mandelbaum
   C. Mrs. Motnowa
   D. Tosha

5. **What makes Vladek reconsider his black market business operations?**
   A. Anja has a second child
   B. An increase in German patrols
   C. The execution of a friend
   D. A close call with a soldier

6. **Who are the first members of Vladek's family to be taken away by the Nazis?**
   A. Vladek's parents
   B. Richieu and Bibbi
   C. His mother-in-law and father-in-law
   D. Anja's grandparents

7. **At the registration at the stadium, who sends Vladek's father to the "good" side?**
    A. Cousin Mordecai
    B. Mr. Ilzecki
    C. Mandelbaum
    D. Anja's father

8. **Why does Vladek's father cross over to the "bad" side at the stadium registration?**
    A. To help his wife
    B. To help his daughter and her children
    C. To help his youngest son
    D. He is grabbed by a German soldier

9. **Where did Mala's parents die?**
    A. Auschwitz
    B. Buchenwald
    C. Dachau
    D. Bergen Belsen

10. **Why does Mala call and wake up Art early in the morning?**
    A. His father has found Anja's diaries
    B. His father has climbed onto the roof
    C. His father has had a heart attack
    D. His father has had a stroke

11. **What does Mala find that makes Vladek so upset?**
    A. Old photos of Richieu
    B. Old photos of Anja
    C. Anja's diary
    D. An old comic of Art's

12. **Where was Art living three months before his mother killed herself?**
    A. Poland
    B. A mental hospital
    C. Los Angeles
    D. A New England college

13. **Who was the first person to find Anja's body?**
    A. Art
    B. Mala
    C. Uncle Herman
    D. Vladek

14. **After a time, the Jews of Sosnowiec are forced to leave for another village; what is the name of this ghetto?**
    A. Bielsko
    B. Srodula
    C. Zawiercie
    D. Dachau

15. **Who takes Richieu to "safety"?**
    A. Mrs. Kawka
    B. Mr. Ilzecki
    C. Uncle Persis
    D. Mrs. Motonowa

16. **How does Richieu die?**
    A. He starves at Auschwitz
    B. He is struck by a German soldier
    C. He is gassed in Auschwitz
    D. He is poisoned by his aunt

17. **Where is Vladek's first hidden bunker?**
    A. Underneath a coal bin
    B. Behind a pile of shoes
    C. In a garbage pile
    D. In the attic, above a chandelier

18. **What job does Haskel provide for Vladek?**
    A. A tin shop
    B. A carpentry shop
    C. A shoe repair shop
    D. A textile factory

19. **What is the accidental ingredient in Pesach's cake?**
    A. Sawdust
    B. Sand
    C. Spoiled milk
    D. Laundry soap

20. **How does Pesach meet his end?**
    A. Typhus at Auschwitz
    B. Gunned down by German guards
    C. Hung for black market activities
    D. Gassed in Auschwitz

21. **What is in Vladek's security deposit box?**
    A. Anja's diaries
    B. Valuables from his marriage with Anja
    C. Cash
    D. Stock certificates

22. **How much is Mala's monthly allowance?**
    A. $0
    B. $50
    C. $25
    D. $100

23. **Where do Anja and Vladek stay during their first night back in Sosnowiec after escaping from the ghetto?**
    A. Mrs. Motonowa's
    B. Mrs. Kawka's
    C. Mr. Ilzecki's
    D. Mr. Lubowski's

24. **Where does Vladek meet Mrs. Motonowa?**
    A. The black market
    B. Mrs. Kawka's
    C. The Srodula ghetto
    D. Mr. Lubowski's

25. **To what country do the smugglers promise to bring Vladek and Anja?**
    A. Turkey
    B. Hungary
    C. Spain
    D. Switzerland

Quiz 2 Answer Key

1. **(A)** Mr. Ilzecki
2. **(B)** He sells textiles on the black market
3. **(B)** A tinsmith
4. **(A)** Mr. Ilzecki
5. **(C)** The execution of a friend
6. **(C)** His mother–in–law and father–in–law
7. **(A)** Cousin Mordecai
8. **(B)** To help his daughter and her children
9. **(A)** Auschwitz
10. **(C)** His father has had a heart attack
11. **(D)** An old comic of Art's
12. **(B)** A mental hospital
13. **(D)** Vladek
14. **(B)** Srodula
15. **(C)** Uncle Persis
16. **(D)** He is poisoned by his aunt
17. **(A)** Underneath a coal bin
18. **(C)** A shoe repair shop
19. **(D)** Laundry soap
20. **(B)** Gunned down by German guards
21. **(B)** Valuables from his marriage with Anja
22. **(B)** $50
23. **(D)** Mr. Lubowski's
24. **(A)** The black market
25. **(B)** Hungary

Quiz 3

1. **Who stays at Mrs. Motonowa's house when Vladek and Anja leave?**
   A. Miloch
   B. Mr. Ilzecki
   C. Mandelbaum
   D. Pesach

2. **Francoise is drawn as what kind of animal?**
   A. Dog
   B. Frog
   C. Moose
   D. Mouse

3. **Americans are drawn as which type of animal?**
   A. Cat
   B. Dog
   C. Fish
   D. Frog

4. **When Mala leaves him, what message does Vladek leave his son to ensure that he will call him back?**
   A. His house in Rego Park has burned down
   B. He has had a heart attack
   C. He has had a stroke
   D. He has found Anja's diaries

5. **Where is Vladek staying for the summer?**
   A. The Catskills
   B. The Chesapeake Bay
   C. The New Jersey Shore
   D. The White Mountains

6. **What job does Vladek need help with when Art and Francoise arrive at Vladek's bungalow?**
   A. Making his bed
   B. Fixing a leak in a drain
   C. Grocery shopping
   D. Organizing his financial papers

7. To which concentration camp is Vladek sent?

A. Birkenau

B. Auschwitz

C. Dachau

D. Bergen Belsen

8. What does Mandelbaum lose while in the concentration camp?

A. Belt

B. Shoes

C. Shirt

D. Spoon

9. In what language does Vladek tutor his Polish guard?

A. English

B. Yiddish

C. Russian

D. French

10. What job is the kapo able to get for Vladek?

A. Manual laborer

B. Tinsmith

C. Carpenter

D. Munitions factory worker

11. What game is being played on the hotel patio that Vladek and Art sneak onto?

A. Shuffleboard

B. Backgammon

C. Horseshoes

D. Bingo

12. What does Pavel have a framed picture of on his desk?

A. His son

B. His wife

C. A car

D. A cat

13. **What is the "secret" ingredient in the bread at Auschwitz?**
    A. Sawdust
    B. Ash
    C. Dirt
    D. Laundry soap

14. **What is the name of the camp to which Anja is sent?**
    A. Birkenau
    B. Treblinka
    C. Gross Rosen
    D. Bergen Belsen

15. **Why does Mancie have higher status than the other prisoners?**
    A. She is having an affair with a guard
    B. She bribes the guards
    C. She is French
    D. She is Polish

16. **According to Art, what was at the gate of the Auschwitz camp?**
    A. A welcome sign
    B. A marching band
    C. The Red Cross
    D. An orchestra

17. **What is Vladek doing during his first conversation with Anja at the concentration camp?**
    A. Carrying a large rock
    B. Repairing a shoe
    C. Carrying a barrel of soup
    D. Fixing a roof

18. **What job does Vladek hold at Auschwitz after the tin shop?**
    A. Shoe repairer
    B. English tutor
    C. Manual laborer
    D. Worker in the gas chambers

19. **In what capacity does Anja come to work in Auschwitz?**
    A. Barracks cleaner
    B. Seamstress
    C. Kitchen attendant
    D. Munitions factory worker

20. **How does Vladek arrange for Anja's kapo to treat her well?**
    A. He bribes her with food
    B. He bribes her with cigarettes
    C. He fixes her shoes
    D. He finds her a new uniform

21. **Where does Anja hide when she is caught receiving food from Vladek?**
    A. Under a blanket
    B. In a ditch
    C. Behind a pile of clothes
    D. In a latrine

22. **All together, how long was Vladek in Auschwitz?**
    A. 3 months
    B. 5 months
    C. 10 months
    D. 12 months

23. **What was Vladek's final job as a tinman?**
    A. Fixing the roof of the Auschwitz barracks
    B. Building defenses for the Russian advance
    C. Building a munitions factory
    D. Pulling apart the gas chambers

24. **What is the name of the chemical used in the gas chambers?**
    A. Dioxin
    B. Zyklon B
    C. Mustard Gas
    D. Sarin

25. **What does Vladek do in his sleep?**
    A. Moves his legs like he's running
    B. Talks about Richieu
    C. Moans loudly
    D. Talks about his wife

Quiz 3 Answer Key

1. **(A)** Miloch
2. **(D)** Mouse
3. **(B)** Dog
4. **(B)** He has had a heart attack
5. **(A)** The Catskills
6. **(D)** Organizing his financial papers
7. **(B)** Auschwitz
8. **(D)** Spoon
9. **(A)** English
10. **(B)** Tinsmith
11. **(D)** Bingo
12. **(D)** A cat
13. **(A)** Sawdust
14. **(A)** Birkenau
15. **(A)** She is having an affair with a guard
16. **(D)** An orchestra
17. **(D)** Fixing a roof
18. **(A)** Shoe repairer
19. **(D)** Munitions factory worker
20. **(C)** He fixes her shoes
21. **(A)** Under a blanket
22. **(C)** 10 months
23. **(D)** Pulling apart the gas chambers
24. **(B)** Zyklon B
25. **(C)** Moans loudly

Quiz 4

1. **Approximately how many pills does Vladek take each day?**
   A. 10
   B. 20
   C. 30
   D. 50

2. **Which Allied army is the first to approach Auschwitz?**
   A. British
   B. Russian
   C. Canadian
   D. American

3. **Where does Vladek plan to hide and wait for the camp's evacuation?**
   A. In an attic
   B. In a latrine
   C. In the closet of his kapo's office
   D. Underneath his bed

4. **Where is Vladek taken immediately after Auschwitz is evacuated?**
   A. Birkenau
   B. Buchenwald
   C. Gross Rosen
   D. Bergen Belsen

5. **What item proves particularly useful in the trains to Dachau?**
   A. Blanket
   B. Gold watch
   C. Shoes
   D. Spoon

6. **What does Vladek want to return to the grocery store?**
   A. Half–eaten boxes of food
   B. Food from another store
   C. Stale bread
   D. Spoiled milk

7. **What disease does Vladek contract in Dachau?**
    A. Typhus
    B. Cholera
    C. Gangrene
    D. Dysentery

8. **What must prisoners in Dachau present to the guards in order to receive soup?**
    A. Their shoes
    B. Their shirt
    C. Their spoons
    D. A bribe

9. **Who does Vladek meet in Dachau that provides him with extra food?**
    A. A gypsy
    B. Mr. Ilzecki
    C. A Frenchman
    D. Mandelbaum

10. **What does Vladek do to land in the infirmary?**
    A. Purposefully cuts his hand
    B. Breaks his own finger
    C. Purposefully cuts his foot
    D. Pretends to have a fever

11. **What does Vladek buy with the extra food he receives from the Frenchman?**
    A. A spoon
    B. New shoes
    C. A new shirt
    D. Cigarettes

12. **Towards which country is Vladek taken to be exchanged as a prisoner of war?**
    A. Sweden
    B. Russia
    C. Switzerland
    D. France

13. **What angers Vladek on the drive back from the grocery store with Art and Francoise?**
    A. Art says a disparaging word about Richieu
    B. Art presses Vladek for more information about Anja
    C. Francoise picks up a black hitchhiker
    D. Francoise almost crashes the car

14. **What does Vladek encounter after he is released by the Germans?**
    A. A German patrol
    B. A Russian patrol
    C. An Italian patrol
    D. An American patrol

15. **Where do Vladek and Shivek hide to wait for things to die down?**
    A. In a house occupied by a sympathetic German couple
    B. In an empty house
    C. By the side of a lake
    D. In the woods

16. **What do Vladek and Shivek drink that makes them so sick?**
    A. Milk
    B. Wine
    C. Vodka
    D. Water

17. **What does Vladek find in his house that he thinks will interest Art?**
    A. Vladek's own diary
    B. Old family photos
    C. Anja's diary
    D. A family tree

18. **Out of Vladek's six siblings, how many survived the holocaust?**
    A. 1
    B. 3
    C. 4
    D. 5

19. **Where does Mala move after she ends her relationship with Vladek?**
    A. Israel
    B. The Catskills
    C. Florida
    D. Brooklyn

20. **What does Art arrange to have waiting for his father when they arrive in New York?**
    A. A new apartment closer to Art's
    B. A completed copy of the first Maus book
    C. A permanent live–in nurse
    D. An ambulance

21. **To what country does Vladek move directly after the war?**
    A. Sweden
    B. United States
    C. United Kingdom
    D. France

22. **How does Vladek support himself after the war?**
    A. He lives off of Anja's parents' inheritance
    B. He regains his old textile factory
    C. He becomes a partner at a department store
    D. He works as a tinsmith

23. **In addition to typhus, what condition does Vladek acquire during the war?**
    A. Hypertension
    B. Cholera
    C. Diabetes
    D. Angina

24. **Where do Vladek and Shivek travel immediately after leaving the displaced persons camp?**
    A. Warsaw
    B. Bielsko
    C. Hannover
    D. Sosnowiec

25. **What name does Vladek call Art just before his nap at the end of the book?**
    A. Shivek
    B. Richieu
    C. Anja
    D. Lolek

Quiz 4 Answer Key

1. **(C)** 30
2. **(B)** Russian
3. **(A)** In an attic
4. **(C)** Gross Rosen
5. **(A)** Blanket
6. **(A)** Half–eaten boxes of food
7. **(A)** Typhus
8. **(B)** Their shirt
9. **(C)** A Frenchman
10. **(A)** Purposefully cuts his hand
11. **(C)** A new shirt
12. **(C)** Switzerland
13. **(C)** Francoise picks up a black hitchhiker
14. **(A)** A German patrol
15. **(B)** In an empty house
16. **(A)** Milk
17. **(B)** Old family photos
18. **(A)** 1
19. **(C)** Florida
20. **(D)** An ambulance
21. **(A)** Sweden
22. **(C)** He becomes a partner at a department store
23. **(C)** Diabetes
24. **(C)** Hannover
25. **(B)** Richieu

ClassicNotes

GrΛdeSaver™

Getting you the grade since 1999™

Other ClassicNotes from GradeSaver™

1984
Absalom, Absalom
Adam Bede
The Adventures of Augie
   March
The Adventures of
   Huckleberry Finn
The Adventures of Tom
   Sawyer
The Aeneid
Agamemnon
The Age of Innocence
Alice in Wonderland
All My Sons
All Quiet on the Western
   Front
All the King's Men
All the Pretty Horses
The Ambassadors
American Beauty
Angela's Ashes
Animal Farm
Anna Karenina
Antigone
Antony and Cleopatra
Aristotle's Ethics
Aristotle's Poetics
Aristotle's Politics
As I Lay Dying
As You Like It
The Awakening
Babbitt
The Bacchae
Bartleby the Scrivener
The Bean Trees
The Bell Jar

Beloved
Benito Cereno
Beowulf
Billy Budd
Black Boy
Bleak House
Bluest Eye
The Bonfire of the
   Vanities
Brave New World
Breakfast at Tiffany's
Call of the Wild
Candide
The Canterbury Tales
Cat's Cradle
Catch-22
The Catcher in the Rye
The Caucasian Chalk
   Circle
The Cherry Orchard
The Chosen
A Christmas Carol
Chronicle of a Death
   Foretold
Civil Disobedience
Civilization and Its
   Discontents
A Clockwork Orange
The Color of Water
The Color Purple
Comedy of Errors
Communist Manifesto
A Confederacy of
   Dunces
Confessions

Connecticut Yankee in
   King Arthur's Court
Coriolanus
The Count of Monte
   Cristo
Crime and Punishment
The Crucible
Cry, the Beloved
   Country
The Crying of Lot 49
Cymbeline
Daisy Miller
Death in Venice
Death of a Salesman
The Death of Ivan Ilych
Democracy in America
Devil in a Blue Dress
The Diary of Anne Frank
Disgrace
Divine Comedy-I:
   Inferno
A Doll's House
Don Quixote Book I
Don Quixote Book II
Dr. Faustus
Dr. Jekyll and Mr. Hyde
Dracula
Dubliners
East of Eden
Emma
Ender's Game
Endgame
Ethan Frome
The Eumenides
Everything is Illuminated
Fahrenheit 451

For our full list of over 250 Study Guides, Quizzes,
Sample College Application Essays, Literature Essays and E-texts, visit:

www.gradesaver.com

ClassicNotes

Gr**A**deSaver™

Getting you the grade since 1999™

Other ClassicNotes from GradeSaver™

The Fall of the House of
Usher
Farewell to Arms
The Federalist Papers
For Whom the Bell Tolls
The Fountainhead
Frankenstein
Franny and Zooey
Glass Menagerie
The God of Small Things
The Grapes of Wrath
Great Expectations
The Great Gatsby
Hamlet
The Handmaid's Tale
Hard Times
Heart of Darkness
Hedda Gabler
Henry IV (Pirandello)
Henry IV Part 1
Henry IV Part 2
Henry V
The Hobbit
Homo Faber
House of Mirth
House of the Seven
Gables
The House of the Spirits
House on Mango Street
Howards End
A Hunger Artist
I Know Why the Caged
Bird Sings
An Ideal Husband
Iliad

The Importance of Being
Earnest
In Our Time
Inherit the Wind
Invisible Man
The Island of Dr. Moreau
Jane Eyre
Jazz
The Joy Luck Club
Julius Caesar
Jungle of Cities
Kidnapped
King Lear
Last of the Mohicans
Leviathan
Libation Bearers
The Lion, the Witch and
the Wardrobe
Lolita
Long Day's Journey Into
Night
Lord Jim
Lord of the Flies
The Lord of the Rings:
The Fellowship of the
Ring
The Lord of the Rings:
The Return of the
King
The Lord of the Rings:
The Two Towers
A Lost Lady
The Love Song of J.
Alfred Prufrock
Lucy
Macbeth

Madame Bovary
Manhattan Transfer
Mansfield Park
MAUS
The Mayor of
Casterbridge
Measure for Measure
Medea
Merchant of Venice
Metamorphoses
The Metamorphosis
Middlemarch
Midsummer Night's
Dream
Moby Dick
Moll Flanders
Mother Courage and Her
Children
Mrs. Dalloway
Much Ado About
Nothing
My Antonia
Native Son
Night
No Exit
Notes from Underground
O Pioneers
The Odyssey
Oedipus Rex / Oedipus
the King
Of Mice and Men
The Old Man and the Sea
On Liberty
One Day in the Life of
Ivan Denisovich

For our full list of over 250 Study Guides, Quizzes,
Sample College Application Essays, Literature Essays and E-texts, visit:

www.gradesaver.com

ClassicNotes

Getting you the grade since 1999™

Other ClassicNotes from GradeSaver™

One Flew Over the Cuckoo's Nest
One Hundred Years of Solitude
Oroonoko
Othello
Our Town
Pale Fire
Paradise Lost
A Passage to India
The Pearl
The Picture of Dorian Gray
Poems of W.B. Yeats: The Rose
Portrait of the Artist as a Young Man
Pride and Prejudice
Prometheus Bound
Pudd'nhead Wilson
Pygmalion
Rabbit, Run
A Raisin in the Sun
The Real Life of Sebastian Knight
Red Badge of Courage
The Republic
Richard II
Richard III
The Rime of the Ancient Mariner
Robinson Crusoe
Roll of Thunder, Hear My Cry
Romeo and Juliet
A Room of One's Own

A Room With a View
Rosencrantz and Guildenstern Are Dead
Salome
The Scarlet Letter
Secret Sharer
Sense and Sensibility
A Separate Peace
Shakespeare's Sonnets
Siddhartha
Silas Marner
Sir Gawain and the Green Knight
Sister Carrie
Six Characters in Search of an Author
Slaughterhouse Five
Snow Falling on Cedars
The Social Contract
Something Wicked This Way Comes
Song of Roland
Sons and Lovers
The Sorrows of Young Werther
The Sound and the Fury
Spring Awakening
The Stranger
A Streetcar Named Desire
The Sun Also Rises
Tale of Two Cities
The Taming of the Shrew
The Tempest
Tender is the Night

Tess of the D'Urbervilles
Their Eyes Were Watching God
Things Fall Apart
The Threepenny Opera
The Time Machine
Titus Andronicus
To Build a Fire
To Kill a Mockingbird
To the Lighthouse
Treasure Island
Troilus and Cressida
Turn of the Screw
Twelfth Night
Ulysses
Uncle Tom's Cabin
Utopia
A Very Old Man With Enormous Wings
The Visit
Volpone
Waiting for Godot
Waiting for Lefty
Walden
Washington Square
Where the Red Fern Grows
White Fang
White Noise
White Teeth
Who's Afraid of Virginia Woolf
Winesburg, Ohio
The Winter's Tale
Woyzeck
Wuthering Heights

For our full list of over 250 Study Guides, Quizzes,
Sample College Application Essays, Literature Essays and E-texts, visit:

www.gradesaver.com

ClassicNotes

GrAdeSaver™

Getting you the grade since 1999™

Other ClassicNotes from GradeSaver™

The Yellow Wallpaper
Yonnondio: From the
    Thirties

For our full list of over 250 Study Guides, Quizzes,
Sample College Application Essays, Literature Essays and E-texts, visit:

www.gradesaver.com

2739391